continue to grow your online presence. I can't recommend it highly enough. If you're serious about taking your business to the next level, this book is a must-have."

-Dexter Jao, Mortgage Agent, The Mortgage Coach

"Astrid has been my go-to tech resource for all things funnel related for years – but now anyone can benefit from her wealth of knowledge! ***SALES FUNNEL MASTERY*** is the perfect resource for digital marketing beginners, giving you literally all the ins and outs of creating your first –or fourth, or fortieth – funnel. Whether you're an entrepreneur carving out your marketing for the first time, or a new digital marketer or student looking for a great resource that provides smart, concise definitions, tips, and tricks for every element of a successful funnel, ***SALES FUNNEL MASTERY*** will get you there."

-Tamara Glick, Personal & Digital Brand Strategist and Aligned Leadership Coach

# PRAISE FOR SALES FUNNEL MASTERY

"*SALES FUNNEL MASTERY* is so much more than a blueprint for building effective sales funnels. The author offers an education that touches on foundational marketing principles, business savvy, tech and platform recommendations, along with clarity on the do's and don'ts of content creation. The purpose of building a funnel is to attract paying customers, so you can deliver value and grow your business. This book delivers effective strategies, tactics, and recommendations for best practices that will deliver top performance again and again. It won't be long before you go from feeling like a novice to successfully increasing your customer base and your bank account."

-**Lisa McGrath, Founder, Strategist, and Entrepreneur Coach, CAVEA Studio Inc.**

"Astrid's *SALES FUNNEL MASTERY* made me realize from start to finish what I needed to do step-by-step to successfully launch my course and offerings. It's both elaborate and straight to the point, making me realize where my strengths are and where to outsource other areas I know would save me time. The examples and planning worksheets made it easy to get started and kept me accountable along the way. Highly recommended for anyone thinking of launching an offering or online program."

-**Silvia Silva, Photographer and CEO, Anchor Studio**

"As an editor, I get to read a lot of great books, but as an editor who also owns a business, I will be returning to this book as a resource again and again. In a clear, comprehensive format, this guide walks you step-by-step through how to turn people from casual shoppers into enthusiastic loyal clients and customers. It has easy-to-follow insights, resources, and maps for designing your own funnels (worth the price of the book alone). Used together with the accompanying worksheets, this book teaches you not only about how funnels work but also walks you through designing and implementing your own straight away, which is invaluable. If you own a business and want to grow, this book is a game-changer."

-Jenna Kalinsky, Founding Director, One Lit Place

"Astrid is a tech unicorn – she knows her stuff – she researches and tests to provide the best solutions to her clients. Her new book combines both her sales expertise and love for her tech into a comprehensive easy-to-use guide on how to get your sales funnel off the ground. **SALES FUNNEL MASTERY** even comes with invaluable worksheets that help you map out the whole process. Although I have some familiarity with sales funnels, I had no idea that there were so many different types. The book was also a great reminder on how important it is to set up sales funnels to scale your business. This book is a must-read for anyone ready to grow their business at any stage of the game."

-**Michelle Daides, CEO & Chief Storyteller, Maverick Makers Content Creation Collective**

"The *SALES FUNNEL MASTERY* book is an absolute game-changer for anyone seeking to elevate their business. Astrid's expertise shines through every page, providing clear, actionable guidance on crafting an effective online sales funnel. With her wealth of knowledge and straightforward approach, Astrid makes complex concepts easy to understand and implement. This book isn't just a one-time read—it's a valuable resource that you'll refer back to time and time again as you

# SALES FUNNEL MASTERY

## Your Step-by-Step Blueprint to Launching Your Products and Services with Success

Astrid Sucipto

Copyright © 2024 by Astrid Sucipto and Digital Pixie

All rights reserved.

No portion of this book may be reproduced in any form without written permission from the publisher or author, except as permitted by U.S. and Canada copyright law.

This publication is designed to provide accurate and authoritative information in regard to the subject matter covered. It is sold with the understanding that neither the author nor the publisher is engaged in rendering legal, investment, accounting or other professional services. While the publisher and author have used their best efforts in preparing this book, they make no representations or warranties with respect to the accuracy or completeness of the contents of this book and specifically disclaim any implied warranties of merchantability or fitness for a particular purpose. No warranty may be created or extended by sales representatives or written sales materials. The advice and strategies contained herein may not be suitable for your situation. You should consult with a professional when appropriate. Neither the publisher nor the author shall be liable for any loss of profit or any other commercial damages, including but not limited to special, incidental, consequential, personal, or other damages.

Book Cover by Author
Publisher: Zeveri Press
Editor: One Lit Place

First edition 2024
www.digitalpixie.ca

ISBN:
Paperback: 978-1-7382803-0-8
Hardcover: 978-1-7382803-2-2
e-book: 978-1-7382803-1-5

# TABLE OF CONTENTS

PRAISE FOR SALES FUNNEL MASTERY ................................. i
PREFACE ................................................................................ ix
JOIN OUR MAILING LIST .................................................... xv
THE GUIDE - WHAT'S INCLUDED: ....................................... 1
    Chapter 1: Know Your Audience ................................................ 7
    Chapter 2: The Basics of a Sales Funnel ................................... 15
    Chapter 3: Funnel Types ............................................................ 27
    Chapter 4: Components of a Sales Funnel ............................... 33
    Chapter 5: The 3 Characteristics of a Great Lead Magnet ........ 41
    Chapter 6: 14 Freebie (Lead Magnet) Ideas ............................. 45
    Chapter 7: Guide to Landing Pages .......................................... 57
    Chapter 8: Types of Landing Pages ........................................... 71
    Chapter 9: Landing Page Copy .................................................. 81
    Chapter 10: Comparison: Landing Page Platforms ................... 87
    Chapter 11: Nurture Emails: What, Why, How, and When? ..... 97
    Chapter 12: Comparison: Email Marketing Tools ................... 113
    Chapter 13: Online Courses ..................................................... 129
    Chapter 14: Comparison: Online Course Platforms ............... 133
    Chapter 15: Other Tech Considerations .................................. 145
    Chapter 16: A/B Testing ........................................................... 157
    Chapter 17: Generating Traffic ................................................ 165
    Chapter 18: Funnel Maps ........................................................ 171
    Chapter 19: Recommended Resources ................................... 181
ACKNOWLEDGMENTS ....................................................... 193
ABOUT THE AUTHOR ........................................................ 197

# PREFACE

## In the Beginning…

Before I started as a funnel tech expert and marketing strategist, I had no idea how to build a funnel or even what it was. I knew having a sales funnel was key for a business because sales funnels are how you guide potential customers to ultimately want to buy what you're selling. But what that series of steps was and how to design each step so people would go from being aware of my products and services to realizing how what I was selling would make their lives better—and further, making a purchase—was a mystery.

Like many entrepreneurs in the early stages of their businesses, I was on a limited budget. Instead of paying a funnel expert, I muddled through building them on my own. What made matters harder was there weren't many (or any, really) Do-It-Yourself (DIY) sales funnel guides on the market I could refer to. I watched lots of webinars and signed up for courses here and there. But no matter how many resources I looked at, nothing provided the clear step-by-step process I needed.

Throughout my journey, I made mistakes that led me to learning valuable lessons, but the mistakes cost a lot of time, energy, and potential revenue. I vowed that my own clients would never have to face the same challenges. As I honed my skills, I began offering my funnel-building services to clients, building a wide range of funnels for different businesses, from simple to advanced.

## Why I Wrote This Book

If you are just starting out or have attempted to set up your own funnel without much success, this book is tailor-made for you. It's designed to save you time, prevent costly mistakes, and alleviate the headaches that come with funnel creation. The truth is you need a strategy and a well-thought-out plan in order for your funnel to be successful, which is precisely what this guide provides. Jam-packed with detailed information, exercises to get you thinking about your own funnel, and associated worksheets (available to you at a discounted rate), this book will help you launch your course, program, product, or service with confidence and purpose.

The book provides the "how-to" information on funnel building. It consists of detailed information and practical hands-on suggestions for creating your own funnels that are the product of my own thousands of hours of setting up funnels for clients and assisting them with their launches. The technical advice is broken down and specific to help you plan your funnel from beginning to end, walking you through the many details you'll need so you make far fewer mistakes and avoid the dead ends someone just starting out would typically experience. It's also meant to help you through, or around, the challenges and hold your hand during the process to ensure you feel strong and prepared for your launch.

## How To Use This Book

You will see that the information in this book is comprehensive, and there's a lot to digest. I recommend that you take your time and maintain realistic expectations.

The book is written to be a useful and valuable tool on its own; however, to get the most out of the learning, you can use my Launch Plan Worksheets, which are designed as a companion tool that walks you through creating your own funnels step-by-step.

When used in conjunction with this book, the Launch Plan Worksheets enable you to not only learn about funnels but to implement the learning in a relevant context to you and your business. Now that you have purchased this book, you can get the worksheets for only $17, which is a 35% discount off the regular price. To access the worksheets, head over to digitalpixie.ca/worksheets or scan the QR code here and use the code "MochaLatte" to receive your discount.

## Keeping Realistic and Getting Ready

Ultimately, while your funnel will have the potential for great success, it may require some adjustments along the way. Funnel design is a process, and over time, your funnel will need to be adjusted to ensure it becomes the perfect marketing approach that targets your exact audience.

The key word here is *process*. You will always encounter people who will guarantee overnight success or promise that by following their plan you'll earn a million dollars with your first launch. Rest assured, I'm not one of them. I want you to be aware that building and refining your funnel will take some time. But that time will become one of the best investments you can make for your business.

Many years ago, I helped a client with her first funnel. She had built an online course but wasn't sure how to get people to sign up for it. We discussed many different approaches, and in the end, she chose to host a webinar as her lead magnet (webinars are excellent lead magnets, which I talk about later in the book). At the end of the webinar, she sold her course to ten people, earning $5,000. Not a life-changing sum for an already-thriving business, but for her just starting out, this was a huge success. She then went on to set up more funnels for additional courses, adjusting and adapting along the way. She now makes multiple six figures a year.

Ultimately, you can trust that with a little patience and a lot of care, you will end up with a thoughtfully crafted sales funnel that will enhance your ability to convert potential leads into paying customers.

Now, are you ready to dive in and change the scope of your business forever? Great. Let's begin!

# JOIN OUR MAILING LIST

This book is a valuable resource and will give you a great foundation for you to understand sales funnels and how to use them to generate leads and turn them into paying customers.

However, because technology is constantly changing, I can guarantee that almost from the time of this book's publication, new platforms, technologies, and systems that help streamline and enhance the funnel-building process will already be on the market.

I am committed to keeping business owners as up-to-date and aware of their options as possible and continuously post the latest advances in funnel-building information and technology. By subscribing to my mailing list, you will be able to continue to build on your own knowledge of funnels and keep current on everything that's working for other entrepreneurs.

Join our mailing list by going to digitalpixie.ca/mailinglist or by scanning the QR code.

# THE GUIDE - WHAT'S INCLUDED:

## 1. Know Your Audience

Knowing your audience is crucial to the success of your business and your funnel. In this chapter, we identify the difference between a target client and a target audience.

## 2. The Basics of a Sales Funnel

Before you get started, you need to understand what a sales funnel is. This chapter breaks it all down for you.

## 3. Funnel Types

In this chapter, we provide an overview of the different funnel types you can create.

## 4. Components of a Sales Funnel

Now that you understand what a sales funnel is, this chapter outlines all the things you need to create one.

## 5. The 3 Characteristics of a Great Lead Magnet

You'll want to create a lead magnet that your target customers actually need. A great lead magnet encourages customers to exchange their valuable information (their email address!) for your offer.

## 6. 14 Freebie Ideas

Review 14 lead magnet ideas with examples of how you can apply them in different businesses.

## 7. Guide to Landing Pages

What makes a landing page great? There's a science to landing pages, and this chapter explores the elements that must be present if you want your landing page to convert.

## 8. Types of Landing Pages

There are different types of landing pages. Understanding each of the different types will help you create a better-converting landing page.

## 9. Landing Page Copy

Don't underestimate the power of your landing page content. Having great copy that converts is essential to your landing page's success (or lack of).

## 10. Comparison: Landing Page Platforms

You'll have to decide on a landing page platform. This chapter goes over the pros and cons of some of the more popular stand-alone landing page platforms as well as provides a comparison chart.

## 11. Nurture Emails: What, Why and How

In this section, we go through the what, why, and how of nurture emails to ensure maximized conversions. We'll also discuss the feelings you want to tap into in your emails.

## 12. Comparison: Email Marketing Tools

A main component of a sales funnel is a drip campaign, and to make this happen, you need an email marketing automation tool. We'll touch on the pros and cons of several of the most popular platforms.

## 13. Online Courses

Online courses are becoming more and more popular. In this chapter, we briefly discuss what an online course is, why individuals prefer online courses, and why entrepreneurs choose to create their own online courses.

## 14. Comparison: Online Course Platforms

If you decide to create an online course as part of your strategy, you'll have to decide how you want to deliver your course. This chapter compares several of the most popular platforms where you can host your online course.

## 15. Other Tech Considerations

There are other tech/systems you might need in order to complete or make your funnel work, such as webinar platforms and checkout tools. In this chapter, we'll discuss what these additional systems are and how to use them.

## 16. A/B Testing

Great marketers are always A/B testing their landing pages and emails. In this chapter, we go over what A/B testing is and why you should consider A/B testing.

## 17. Generating Traffic

After you've built your funnel, you need to drive traffic to it. Here, we review different ways you can drive traffic to your landing page.

## 18. Funnel Maps

Now that you know the different types of funnels you can create, this chapter provides a funnel workflow visual for each type of funnel.

## 19. Resources

We created a list of recommended resources to help you put your plan into action.

# 20. Launch Plan Worksheets (Recommended)

In this final chapter, we will discuss the importance of having a launch plan and what's included in our Launch Plan Worksheets.

# Chapter 1: Know Your Audience

In every business, it's critical that you identify and get to know your audience. Knowing your audience best equips you to laser-target your marketing efforts, including your marketing funnel. In a sales funnel, "audience" refers to a group of people who have been targeted and who have engaged with you as potential customers.

Note: A "target audience" is different from a "target market." They are related and often used interchangeably, but they have distinct meanings in marketing. Let's review the difference between these two terms.

## Target Market

Target market refers to the broader group of people that a company wants to reach with its products and services. This group may include various customer segments, and each segment may have its own distinct target audience. For example, a mortgage company's target market will be anyone who needs a mortgage. Within this target market, there can be various segments and audiences. Let's take a look at what that means.

## Target Audience

Target audience is a specific group of individuals who are the focus of a marketing campaign or message. The target audience represents a more narrowly defined segment of the overall market. The target audience is characterized by shared characteristics, interests, behaviors, demographics, or needs that make the people more likely to be interested in a particular product or service. Identifying a target audience helps marketers tailor their communication and advertising efforts to resonate with this specific group, increasing the likelihood of engagement and conversion.

Continuing with the previous example of a mortgage business, the target market could be further segmented into first-time home buyers, property investors, those looking to downsize, those looking to refinance their mortgages, those who want to pay off their mortgage as quickly as possible, etc.

You can target these broader audiences within the market, or you can segment them even further; for example, the target audience can be first-time home buyers who are looking for a condominium (as opposed to a house) in a specific area.

What will help you to most effectively build your funnel so it is tailored exactly to your audience's needs is to create an audience avatar (also known as a buyer persona or ideal representative). This avatar is a detailed fictional representation of your ideal customer and embodies the demographic information such as age, gender, location, income level, education, and occupation, as well as psychographic details like interests, values, beliefs, challenges, goals, and buying behaviors of your ideal customer. Like a real person, your customer avatar can fall into one or more customer segments. Importantly, you will want to create them in full so you can see them (it may even help to give your avatar a name).

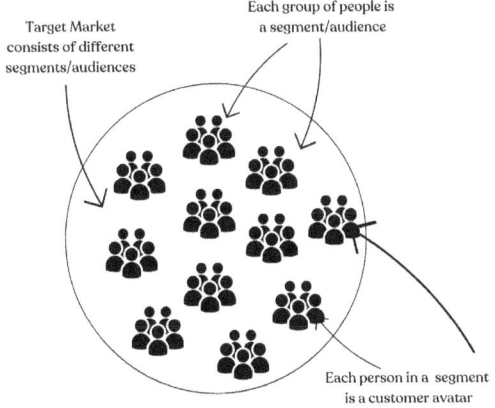

# It Is Critical That You Know Your Target Audience Before Building Your Funnel For Several Reasons

## Specific and Targeted Communication

Understanding your target audience allows you to tailor your marketing messages, content, and advertising to resonate with your audience's specific needs, preferences, and pain points (issues or situations they want to solve or fix). When your messaging aligns with what your audience cares about, they are more likely to pay attention and engage with your brand.

## More Efficient Marketing Efforts

Identifying your target audience helps allocate your marketing resources more effectively. Instead of spreading your efforts thinly across a broad market, you can focus on the segments most likely to convert. This optimization leads to better return on investment (ROI) and maximizes the impact of your marketing spend.

## Improved Product Development

Knowing your target audience enables you to gain insights into your audience's preferences, desires, and challenges. This information can be used to develop products or services that better meet their needs, leading to higher customer satisfaction and loyalty.

## Better Connection With Your Customers

Tailoring your marketing to your target audience fosters a sense of connection and understanding. Customers are more likely to feel that your brand "gets" them, which can strengthen the relationship between your business and its customers.

## Competitive Advantage

Understanding your target audience allows you to differentiate your brand from competitors. By catering specifically to your audience's unique requirements, you can position your products or services as the preferred choice within that segment.

Going back to the previous example of a mortgage business, by catering to first-time home buyers who are looking for a condominium in a specific area, you'll become the go-to mortgage company for this specific audience.

## More Effective Lead Generation

Aligning your business with your target audience enables you to identify the most effective channels and methods for lead generation. You can focus on platforms and strategies where your target audience is most active, saving time and effort in reaching potential customers.

## Personalization

Personalized marketing experiences are becoming increasingly important to consumers. By knowing your target audience, you can create personalized content and offers that appeal to individual preferences, increasing the likelihood of conversion.

## Customer Retention

Understanding your audience helps you deliver ongoing value to existing customers. Satisfied customers are more likely to remain loyal, make repeat purchases, and recommend your brand to others.

Overall, when you tap into the heart of your target audience, you're best able to create a more relevant, engaging, and impactful marketing strategy and sales funnel. By tailoring your efforts to the audience's specific needs, you can build stronger customer relationships, increase brand loyalty, and achieve better business results.

# Chapter 1 Questions/Exercises

1. Who is your target market and who is your target audience?
_____
_____
_____
_____
_____

2. Why is it important for you to know your target audience?
_____
_____
_____
_____

Again, it's essential you know not only who your target audience is but details about them, which will help you define how you approach them and meet their needs.

For example, if you offer services for bakers, it's not enough to say that your target audience is bakers. You have to know what type of baker they are, what products they sell, who their target audience is, what motivates them to sell to their audience, etc.

For a more detailed exercise on figuring out and getting clear as to who your target audience is, head over to digitalpixie.ca/worksheets and enter code "MochaLatte" to get 35% off the worksheets and use them along with this book.

# Chapter 2: The Basics of a Sales Funnel

## What Is a Sales Funnel?

Simply put, a sales funnel is a system that moves your audience from Point A to Point B: Point A being the starting point and Point B being the destination.

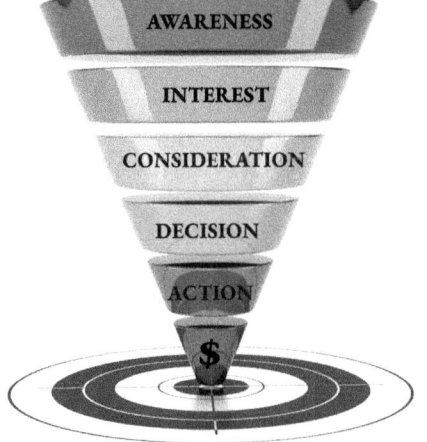

**Point A** is the top or broadest part of the funnel. This is the awareness point where potential customers enter your funnel. The further they go down, the narrower and more specific and targeted the funnel becomes, and the closer they get to Point B.

**Point B** is the very bottom of the funnel, the point where people who are in your funnel are ready to buy. Usually, only a handful of people (about 2-3%) are ready to buy at the beginning, or when they enter your funnel. As a business, you would want to increase that number, so you have more people entering your funnel and therefore a greater number ready to buy by the time they get to the bottom. A good conversion number to aim for at the bottom of the funnel is 3-7%.

The purpose of a sales funnel is two-fold:

1. To warm up your cold leads (a cold lead is people who amble into your funnel to enjoy your free giveaway but who are not interested in buying; are open to buying but don't have an express intention to buy; or are keen to buy as long as what you're selling is right for them).
2. To filter out the people who are not ready to buy either at this time or at all, and to nurture the ones who are inclined to buy so when they get to the bottom, they are 100% in.

The sales "funnel" is a good visual representation of the customer journey as it enables you to see the various steps individuals go through as they warm up to your business before making a purchase or becoming a customer. The funnel is designed to catch the attention of a broad audience at the top and then, as it gradually narrows, moves prospects through the various stages towards conversion.

## The Different Stages of a Sales Funnel

### 1. Awareness

This is the very top of the funnel where you draw in your leads. In this stage, your leads are considered "cold" leads. They don't know much or at all about you or what you offer. One of the best ways to draw them into your funnel is through a blog, a video, or other types of content. In your content, offer advice or solutions to your audience's problem that they can apply right now to help them.

By doing this, you are creating awareness for the topic in which you are an expert. You can also create awareness by showing up where your leads are (for example, in Facebook or LinkedIn groups), and then driving them to your content for more information or directly to your freebie. You can also run social media ads to bring awareness to what you're selling. The goal is to turn your target audience's heads in your direction so they become aware of who you are, what you do, and how you're uniquely positioned to help so you can bring them into your sales funnel.

### 2. Interest

After awareness comes interest. Once your audience is aware of your expertise, you want to hook them in and get them into your funnel. One way to do this is to offer a freebie, which is also called a lead magnet. Your freebie has to be enticing enough that your leads would want to give you their contact info in exchange for your freebie. Here, your copy has to be on point, and having a great landing page is extremely important (more on that later).

Another option other than offering a freebie is to offer a trip wire, which is a low-cost product that is an easier spend for your leads. With this item or service, they get a taste of the kinds of things you offer before making a bigger investment with you.

Tip: If you're just starting out and new to funnels, I would recommend that you offer something for free first because people generally love free offerings. It would be easier for a person to exchange their personal information for something free if they don't know you yet.

This benefits both sides:

1. The person - as they can get to know how you can help them before committing to buy from you
2. You - as it is a great way to build your email list and gain trust from people who don't know you yet.

## 3. Consideration

The consideration stage is an important stage of your funnel. To get to this stage, the audience has already shown interest, which may mean they are considering the product or service you offer as a potential solution to their needs or problems. This is the juncture when you have to truly warm up or nurture these leads to turn them into paying customers as they are still getting to know you and aren't quite ready to trust you in full. Although not impossible, asking them to buy from you right now would likely result in disappointment.

In this stage, the goal is to help your leads understand what you do and how you, your service, or your product can help them solve their problems. You give your leads two choices to make:

1. Take action and buy
2. Ignore your offer and take no action

The goal here is to help them see the benefits of buying your offer and the disadvantages of not taking any action. This can be done through a series of emails, also known as a drip campaign or nurture emails. This is where your customers will consider your offer to take action. This stage helps your customers make a decision and move into the "decision" stage.

## 4. Decision

In the previous consideration stage, you've given your leads all the information they need to make a decision. If your lead is still part of your funnel, they will have likely informed themselves about what you're selling by performing outside research into what's available, compared the options, and are now close to making a decision to purchase. In this decision stage, they are weighing the cost/benefits of your offer so they can make their purchase.

## 5. Action

By the time your leads get to the "action" stage, they have become hot leads. If your consideration and decision stages have been effective, your leads will take the action you want them to take. Because a funnel starts bigger at the top and gets smaller at the bottom, only a small percentage of leads that come into your funnel will be ready to buy at this point. But keep in mind that the other leads who aren't ready to buy will at the very least be warmed up. They may not be ready to buy right now, but they may very well buy at some point in the future. In this action stage, your focus is on turning the people who are ready to buy now, into paying customers.

## 6. Loyalty

By this stage, the leads in your funnel are categorized into two categories:

### A. Those who purchased and became paying customers

After the purchase, the focus shifts to retaining the people who bought as loyal customers. Satisfied customers may become advocates who refer your product or service to others. It is also a lot more cost-effective to market to your existing customers than to get new customers to buy from you. In this stage, you want to keep the interest going and be top of mind. You can do this by keeping in regular contact with your customers, which can be in the form of a regular newsletter, a check-in email, or a check-in phone call.

**B. Those who did not purchase by the time they got to the bottom of the funnel**

For the leads who made it to the bottom of the funnel but still didn't purchase, your marketing doesn't stop here. You can continue to nurture them through regular newsletters or put them through another funnel such as a downsell funnel.

# What Happens Next? Downsells, Upsells, and Product Bumps

You've brought your leads to the bottom of your funnel and have turned them into paying customers. Now what? Do you do the happy dance? (Absolutely!) Do you stop marketing? No, you don't. Although a funnel is typically associated with an upside-down triangle, when it comes to marketing or sales, its behavior is actually more circular because you keep the audience cycling through your funnel.

Whether your leads end up being paying customers or not, you should continue to nurture them and offer them valuable information. You'll want to separate your leads into two groups:

1. Leads that turned into paying customers. Continuing to provide them with valuable information will keep them coming back to you and eventually purchase from you again, becoming repeat customers.
2. Leads who didn't buy from you. Continuing to provide your leads with valuable information will eventually turn them into paying customers.

In addition to keeping in touch with your leads and existing customers through regular newsletters at the end of a sales funnel, let's look at a few strategies that can keep your funnel going in order to maximize revenue and customer conversion during the buying process.

## Downsells

For the leads who ended up at the bottom of the funnel but didn't buy, you have the option to move them through another funnel with an offering that might be less expensive. For example, if your initial lead magnet was a freebie that led to a paid product they didn't buy, you might want to move them to a tripwire funnel (a low-cost offer). This is called a "downsell."

If these leads have shown interest all along: they've opened your emails, they've clicked on the links in your email, they've even clicked on the sales page, but they still haven't bought, they might not be ready to buy yet. In this situation, you can offer them something low cost and easy to buy to give them a taste of what it's like to work with you and how you can help them.

In other words, a downsell is a strategy used when a customer declines the initial offer or upsell. Instead of losing the sale entirely, you can offer a less expensive alternative or a different product that still meets the customer's needs. The idea is to offer a more budget-friendly option that might be appealing enough to convince the customer to complete the purchase.

## Upsells

An "upsell" is a strategy to encourage a customer who is in the process of buying from you or who has recently bought from you to purchase more items/services, or to purchase a more expensive or upgraded version of the product or service they are interested in or have already added to their cart. Upselling can lead to increased revenue per customer and is an effective way to boost profitability. In the case of your sales funnel, you can move your paying customers through another funnel with another offering that may or may not be entirely related to their recent purchase. Or you can expand the current funnel to get them to buy something else right away.

For example, if they buy an on-demand course, you might want to offer them an upgrade to a course plus one-on-one coaching with you. This is called an "upsell." An upsell happens after the initial sale. It can be immediate such that another page opens with your upsell offering, or there can be a delay whereby the upsell is offered through a series of emails.

## Product Bump

A "product bump" (also known as an order bump or upsell bump) happens during the sale. It is an additional offer displayed at the point of purchase. It happens right after they click "buy" but before they've entered their payment information. It usually appears on the checkout page and is designed to entice customers to add more items to their current order just before they complete the transaction, thereby increasing their cart value.

The product bump is often a related or complementary product that can enhance the customer's experience or solve a problem. You might offer them a workbook or journal for only $5 that's built to accompany your course or a one-time coaching call with you for only $75. It's like going to McDonald's and being asked if you'd like fries with your order. The goal is the same - to increase the purchase value. Keep in mind that whether you can offer a product bump will depend on the tech you're using. For example, product bump is an add-on in Woocommerce requiring the purchase of an extra plugin, while in Thrivecart, the ability to add a product bump is included.

# Word of Caution

If you're a beginner starting with a funnel, let's not dive into the complexities of downsells, upsells, and product bumps just yet. I want you to understand that funnels offer limitless possibilities, but they can be overwhelming for beginners to set up. For now, we'll concentrate on mastering one basic funnel and getting it to work for you!

The most important takeaway with funnels is that you focus on nurturing your leads regardless of whether they become paying customers or not. This is done by continuously sending them valuable and informative emails. This way, when they are ready to make a purchase or consider additional products, they will remember you and your brand. Building a relationship with your audience is essential for long-term success.

# Chapter 2 Questions/Exercises

1. Can you think of a freebie you can offer to grab your leads' attention and get them into your funnel? The freebie should be something that is connected to the end product you'd like to sell.

_____
_____
_____
_____

2. What are some of the things you can do to create awareness of your freebie? (Stage #1)?

_____
_____
_____
_____

3. What do you hope to happen by getting people to sign up for your freebie and enter your funnel?

_____
_____
_____
_____

Go even deeper into your planning with the Launch Plan Worksheets, available at digitalpixie.ca/worksheets (enter code "MochaLatte").

# Chapter 3: Funnel Types

Before you start planning your funnel, you'll want to know what the different types of funnels are. This will help you decide what type of funnel you'd like to create and what you want it to achieve.

## List Building Funnel

A list building funnel is the simplest type of funnel. It involves offering a lead magnet in exchange for your leads' contact details for the purpose of building your list. Once they're part of your list, you can nurture your leads via email and nudge them to take action such as book a consultation with you or purchase something from you.

## Free Consultation Funnel

This funnel involves a series of emails that nudge your leads toward signing up for a free consultation. During the consultation, you can upsell your product or service. If they didn't sign up for a free consultation, you can continue to nurture them via email and possibly add them into a different funnel in the future.

## Product Launch Funnel

When you launch a new product, you can create a funnel that is focused on educating your leads about your new product. This product can be a physical product or a digital product such as an online course.

## Webinar Funnel

A webinar funnel attracts leads via a webinar (live or automated). It involves offering a free training in exchange for your leads' contact details. The purpose of a webinar funnel is more than just to build your list; it also enables you to sell your product or service at the end of the funnel. The funnel involves sending your lead reminders before the webinar, making the offer during the webinar (optional), and following up with a series of emails after the webinar.

## The Waitlist Funnel

This funnel builds excitement for your product launch. It involves asking people to sign up for the waitlist so they are first to be notified when the product launches. This is used if there is going to be a limit to the number of products or registrations available. It creates demand and a sense of urgency.

## The Mini Course Funnel

The mini course funnel involves offering a series of video training—a mini version of your main course—and is usually free or low cost. It gives your leads a glimpse of what your higher paid course would be like while giving them just enough information to be helpful but not too much, leaving them wanting more.

## The Abandoned Cart Funnel

This funnel is meant to re-capture any lost leads that were close to buying your product but didn't. The purpose is to remind them about the benefits of the product they were about to buy and nudge them towards making the purchase.

## The Post-Purchase Funnel

The post-purchase funnel is more of an email sequence than a funnel (but it can be turned into a funnel when you combine it with other funnels). This is a sequence that you send out after a customer buys your product or service. It consists of a confirmation email and any other details the customer may need to know about their purchase. For example, if your customer signed up for an online course consisting of many modules, you can send out an email every time a module opens up. If you've included a weekly coaching call, you can include a reminder email with details to prepare them for the call.

You can also take the opportunity to cross-sell or upsell your products or services. When you cross-sell or upsell your products, you are now putting the customer through another funnel.

## The Downsell Funnel

When your leads don't end up buying the product, it could be that they're not ready to buy yet or not ready to spend the money on your product. The downsell funnel puts those leads into another funnel that offers an alternative product at a much lower cost that is more digestible for them, while still solving their problem. The idea is that the cost is low enough for them to justify spending so they get a taste of what it would be like to work with you. It also gets them more comfortable with the idea of eventually spending the money on the higher cost product.

## The Upsell Funnel

The upsell funnel is usually done as an expansion of the Product Launch Funnel. For example, if the product is an evergreen digital course, you could offer a few one-on-one coaching sessions with you as an upsell. This funnel happens after the purchase of the product.

## Deadline Funnel

A deadline funnel is a funnel that has an expiry or a deadline. Having a deadline creates a sense of urgency and instills the fear of missing out. You can use a deadline funnel to offer a discount or to simply close the offer.

## Evergreen Funnel

An evergreen funnel is a funnel that you set up once, and it runs continuously. You can turn any of the above funnels into an evergreen although the term is mostly used for automated webinar funnels.

## Funnel Maps

In Chapter 18, you'll see visual representations of the funnels, which are referred to as funnel maps.

# Chapter 3 Questions/Exercises

1. Do you have something that you want to sell through your funnel, or are you just building your list for now?

_____
_____
_____
_____

2. Now that you know the different funnel types available, what type of funnel will you be starting with? Why did you choose this funnel type?

_____
_____
_____
_____

# Chapter 4: Components of a Sales Funnel

Now that you have a good understanding of what a sales funnel is, it's time to learn what you need to put one together. A sales funnel has the following key components:

## 1. Lead / Email Capture

We learned in the previous section that you create awareness and interest for people who may be interested in you at the top of the funnel. But how do you ... funnel them into a funnel? By using a lead capture! This is often done using a form (called an opt-in form) that asks your leads for their name and email address in exchange for some valuable information that you've promised you'll give them (your lead magnet). Having a form is essential; without it, you can't build your list and nurture your leads.

There are several platforms you can use to create your form. Most email marketing platforms offer the ability to create a form. Your website platform might also offer some type of form builder.

My recommendation is to use the email marketing and website platform MailerLite (https://digitalpixie.ca/resources/mailerlite), but you can use anything else that works for you.

Tip: at the back of this book, you'll find a resource section that contains links to the various tech/systems I recommend.

## GDPR

Before we move on to the next section, I wanted to touch briefly on GDPR (General Data Protection Regulation) requirements, which state that in order for you to send emails to people, they first must opt-in. Otherwise, emails you send are considered spam, which is highly frowned upon and can even get you in some hot water (in the most severe case, you could be fined up to 20 million euros). The opt-in process also needs to be thorough; it's not enough for people to enter their name and email on a form and click "submit." The form they fill out also must have a checkbox they click that confirms their consent to receive emails from you. Without their express permission, you aren't legally allowed to email them.

### Double Opt-In

I also want to touch on double opt-in vs. single opt-in. Double opt-in is a method used to confirm the legitimacy of an email subscriber's consent to receive communications. It involves an additional step after someone signs up for an email list whereby they receive a confirmation email with a unique link or a verification code. The user needs to click the link or enter the code to confirm their subscription. Single opt-in means that the subscriber does not need to confirm their opt-in to receive additional email marketing from you.

Whether or not you should turn on double opt-in is a matter of preference and best practice for your business. On one hand, turning it on ensures that only those who truly want to be on your email list are added. This reduces spam complaints and improves deliverability. On the other hand, the extra step of having to confirm the subscription may cause you to lose subscribers. They might not see the double opt-in request if it lands in their junk or promotions folder, or they might just choose not to bother going the extra step. I will also note that at the time of writing this book, double opt-in is not a requirement of GDPR. Therefore it's a personal decision, and as a business, you'll need to decide if having a double opt-in will benefit you or not.

## 2. Landing Page

A landing page is the page you drive your audience to that houses the lead capture. It can be your website's homepage and your lead capture is a pop-up form. It can also be a specific single page with more information about your lead magnet and an embedded opt-in form. We'll talk more about landing pages in Chapter 7.

## 3. Thank You Page

The thank you page is an often forgotten component. Your sales funnel will not fail if you don't have a thank you page, but this page serves a few purposes:

1. It confirms that the subscriber is now on your list
2. It reminds them to check their email inbox or spam folder for the information they just signed up for
3. It becomes an additional marketing opportunity to drive them to your blog, social media, or some other content such as a short video to keep their interest going

## 4. Email Marketing and Drip Campaign

The next important component of a sales funnel is email marketing. Email marketing is an effective and powerful way to warm up your cold leads. When it comes to funnels, emails are what you use to nurture the leads who just signed up to receive your lead magnet to guide them through the funnel. The series of emails you send them is called a drip campaign or nurture emails. We'll touch on this in more detail in Chapter 11.

## 5. Offer

Typically, a sales funnel leads to an offer. It can be either a paid offer or a free offer that eventually leads to a sale. Remember that the goal of a funnel is to make money from selling your product or service. If you decide to do a paid offer such as an online course, you'll need another landing page called a sales page, where you present information about your offer with a goal of having your leads sign up and buy.

## 6. Checkout Page

From my experience, a checkout page, like a thank you page, is often forgotten as well, but if your end goal is to sell and make money, then the checkout page is a crucial part of your funnel. How are people going to pay for your product? If you don't have a paid offer, or you are simply building your list, a checkout page is not necessary. However, if you want people to purchase your offer, you'll need to bring them somewhere to make that purchase. We'll talk about the various checkout platforms in Chapter 15.

## Do You Have To Have a Paid Offer Ready To Go To Set Up a Funnel?

The short answer is no. If you're just starting out, you might not have a paid offer such as a course, program, or product to sell yet, and that's okay! Many of my clients have been hesitant to set up a funnel because they weren't at the point where they had anything to sell. But don't let the lack of a paid offer deter you from building a sales or marketing funnel.

If you're a coach, for example, while you might not have a course offering, you could offer your coaching services. Instead of taking your leads to a sales page to buy from you, you'd instead guide them to schedule a discovery call with you. During the discovery call, you would sign them up as a coaching client.

Or if you're simply trying to build up your list without having any offers at all (no discovery call, no coaching services, no product, etc.), that's okay too! Building a list is really important for the time when you are ready to launch your product or service because then you will have a warm audience to sell to.

If you're simply building your list and not offering anything, your funnel would stop at the consideration stage. From that point, you'd continue to nurture your leads through regular emails that offer a ton of value for them. When they read your emails and get value, they subconsciously align themselves with you and eventually may consider working with you or buying your product when you have something to sell. By the time you are ready to offer something they can buy, you can easily move them into the next two stages - decision and action.

Keep in mind that the goal of any business is to make money, so eventually, you will need to offer your leads something they can buy.

## Chapter 4 Questions/Exercises

1. Now that you know all the elements that should be present in a sales funnel, what do you feel is the most important element and why?

2. Let's say you are selling a digital product. Which element or elements are important to have in your sales funnel that allows your leads to purchase the product?

3. What are some of the things you would include in your Thank You page?

# Chapter 5: The 3 Characteristics of a Great Lead Magnet

A lead magnet is an incentive you can offer your audience in exchange for their contact information. This magnet helps you build your mailing list and generate leads. The success of your lead magnet will depend on how good it is and the content that follows.

A great lead magnet has the following 3 characteristics:

## ☑ Valuable

For your audience to be attracted to your lead magnet, it has to have perceived value. While people generally love free stuff, most are also overwhelmed with too much information and can be reluctant to give out their contact information unless it is for a very good reason. Your audience has to feel that your offer is something of value to them, something they need that can help with whatever challenges they might be facing.

## ☑ Immediate Solution

Before providing their information, your audience wants to know what's in it for them and how the information is going to help them. They're looking for solutions they can implement immediately to a problem they are facing. If your lead magnet offers that immediate solution, they will gladly give out their email address in exchange for that solution.

## ☑ Your Point of Difference

Also known as your Unique Selling Proposition (USP), the lead magnet should clearly point out what makes you awesome and why your audience should buy from you rather than from your competitors.

Does your lead magnet meet all of the above criteria? If you're not sure, you can always ask a small selection of your audience for an honest review of your lead magnet before you release it to a wider audience. That way, you can also get their opt-in, and when you release it, they will be more likely to recommend your lead magnet to others. You could consider offering something in exchange for their time and honest feedback, such as a free one-hour coaching call or something else as you see fit.

# Chapter 5 Questions/Exercises

1. As a consumer, what would make you give your personal information (name and email) to a business?

___

2. As a consumer, when you see a free offer, what do you look for to help you decide if you should sign up for the offer?

___

# Chapter 6: 14 Freebie (Lead Magnet) Ideas

Each of the ideas below includes an industry-specific example to show how the lead magnet can be applied to different types of businesses. For each idea and example, think of how you could apply it to your own business. What valuable information can you give your audience that would make a great freebie, and why would it be valuable for them?

## 1. Resource List

A resource list works great for many industries. You can compile valuable resources that will help make it easier for your target audience to find the information they need.

**Example:** Ontario's Dazzling Wedding Wonderlands: The 15 Most Magical Venues with Pros and Cons for Every Season!

This lead magnet would be great for a wedding event planning business. A wedding venue is often one of the first items a couple needs to secure, and with so many options, where does one start? By offering a resource list with pros and cons, and perhaps what type of wedding is best for each venue, you can help narrow down the options for an already overwhelmed couple.

## 2. How-To Guide

The time-honored how-to guide is an oldie but goodie. Consumers are always looking for ways to do something better, make it easier, do things properly, etc.

**Example:** Healthy Mom, Healthy Baby: The Ultimate Guide to Mastering the Art of a Nutrient-Rich Diet for Gestational Diabetes.

This guide would be great for nutritionists, dietitians, and any other business that offers nutritional services or products. This lead magnet solves the problem that pregnant people with gestational diabetes face when it comes to balancing meals with their glucose levels—making sure that they are eating enough and enough of the right foods to keep their glucose levels low.

## 3. Expert Tips

As an expert in your industry, you most certainly have a number of helpful tips you could easily rattle off. You might even be doing this already when you meet with people, probably unconsciously. When offering tips in a lead magnet format, use a number. People like numbers. Depending on what that number is, consumers will associate the number as being easy and doable or value-packed.

**Example:** Bye-Bye Back Pain: 3 Easy Stretches to Ease Your Aching Back in Just Minutes a Day.

This lead magnet example is great if you are in the health and wellness industry. This offers value to clients who experience back pain and have a busy life. Three stretches seem very doable, quick, and easy. It's a solution that can be easily incorporated into a busy schedule.

## 4. Webinar

This is also another oldie but goodie. Consumers love free training. They eat up free content. If you have a way to educate your audience about a topic that resonates with them, this is a great lead magnet. The key is to make it valuable enough that they can take what they learn in the webinar and apply it to their business or life, but also show them that by signing up for your paid program, product, or service, you could help them take their work or learning to the next level.

## 5. Checklist

A checklist can work for many different industries. Think about your program, product, or service and find a way to break information down into a digestible checklist. Ask yourself why your audience would need a checklist and how a checklist would make their life easier.

**Example:** Family Adventure Awaits! Don't Leave Home Without It: Your Ultimate Packing Checklist for an Epic Trip with Little Explorers!

This is great if you are a travel agent or work in the travel industry. Packing for yourself is one thing, but packing for the entire family, especially when you have young children, is another. Your target audience could appreciate having a checklist handy to make sure they don't forget anything important for their little ones such as fever and allergy medicines, thermometer, puffers, extra underwear, stuffed animals, and snacks for the car. Checklists are easy for you to create and provide great value for your audience in an easily digestible format.

## 6. Questions / Assessment

This type of lead magnet can also work across multiple industries. The idea is to compile a list of questions to help your audience determine if they are the right fit for something.

**Example:** Ready to Rewrite Your Career Story? 10 Powerful Questions to Consider Before Taking the Leap!

This example is great for businesses in the career industry: career counseling, recruitment services, résumé writing services, career transitions services, second career coaching, etc. If your audience is experiencing the desire to change careers for whatever reason but are still in the unsure stage, they will likely be drawn to this assessment. Questions will help them figure out if they are really ready for a career change and confirm what their gut is telling them, or whether there's another path they can take to solve their career challenges.

## 7. Quiz

This is another lead magnet that can work for almost any industry. With a quiz, you're asking the consumer questions that will guide them to the final verdict, which will potentially help them make a decision. You can use a platform like Interact to build your interactive quiz.

**Example:** Beyond Baby Blues: Unmasking the Shadows - Is Postpartum Depression Knocking at Your Door?

This is great for businesses that work with postpartum patients, keeping in mind that although postpartum depression is generally associated with the birthing person, the partner could also be suffering from depression, especially as a first-time parent. Perhaps you are a therapist who works with families and new parents, or perhaps you are a doula who offers postpartum services. Your target audience would be drawn to a quiz like this even if they have the slightest concern about postpartum depression. Or maybe they want confirmation that what they are feeling is not actually depression but something quite commonly experienced by many new parents.

## 8. Help Questions

This is great for businesses in the e-commerce space or for businesses who want to offer suggestions as to which product or service is best for their audience.

**Example:** Unleash Your Scent-sational Side: Embark on an Aromatic Journey to Find Your Perfect Fragrance!

This type of lead magnet would work well if you're in a business that offers products related to scents such as candles, perfumes, lotions, bubble baths, etc. Think of this as a guide to help your customers choose their perfect scent. The idea is that you're taking them through a series of questions to get to know them better and it ends with you suggesting a couple of options for them. Getting answers to questions such as "Do you like roses or lilacs?" or "Do you like sweet or citrus?" helps you suggest the "perfect scent" for them. Questions help the consumer figure out what they need, which makes it easier for them to make a decision and click that buy button!

## 9. Samples

Samples work great especially for product-based businesses although they can also work well for service-based businesses. Giving away a sample for a physical product can be fairly straightforward.

**For example,** if you sell natural eco-friendly diapers, you might want to give away a pack of two for your customers to try. If you sell a recipe book or a planner, you might want to give away a few recipes as a digital download or the first 30 days of your planner for free.

For service-based businesses, giving away samples can still work; it just looks a little different. If you are a fitness trainer who offers weekly personal training sessions, you could give two free days to "try" your training out and see if you're a good fit for your customer. If you are a coach, you might want to give away a trial session. You could also give out a "sample" by inviting them to a free challenge.

## 10. White Paper

A white paper is a compilation of your research findings on a specific topic. This type of lead magnet might not work for every business. It will, however, work well for businesses that offer some type of consultation.

**Example:** Unleashing the Power of Autonomous Work Environments: The Ultimate White Paper to Boost Employee Productivity!

This lead magnet sample would work great if you're in the Human Resources space and you offer consultation for employee relations and employee productivity. Your target audience who are concerned about their employees' productivity, or who are simply interested in keeping or increasing productivity will want to read the research behind Employee Productivity to get ideas they can apply to increase productivity in their own business.

## 11. An e-book

An e-book is a short book about your topic of expertise. It can work for just about any business. In addition to the written content, you can include tips, questions, checklists, etc.

**Example:** Master the Art of Social Media Marketing: Your Ultimate e-book Guide for Digital Success!

This example is great for businesses that offer social media marketing services. A free e-book is generally a more comprehensive read than an expanded blog and can range anywhere from 10-100 pages. You'll want to find the sweet spot between delivering great value and not giving away too much. The idea is to illuminate your readers while making them aware that this is the tip of the iceberg, and there's much more to learn on this subject, which will cause them to hire you or buy your product.

## 12. Worksheet

A worksheet helps your audience work out their problems into a solution. It can be used as a standalone lead magnet or in combination with another one.

**Example:** Unleash The Author In You: Your Step-by-Step Planning Worksheet for Crafting Your First Masterpiece!

This lead magnet would be ideal for businesses that offer a writing course. People who have a story to tell and want to write a book but don't know where to start would likely be drawn to this lead magnet. Another great example is any of the companion worksheets for this book (you can find all of my Launch Plan Worksheets at digitalpixie.ca/worksheets. Enter code "MochaLatte" to get the discounted rate).

## 13. Video / Mini Course

A video or video series (also known as a mini training/course) can really grab your audience's attention. This can be used for any industry. It is especially good at providing a demo to your audience by giving them a glimpse of your offering.

**Example:** From Idea to Impact: Craft Your Epic Online Course in Just 60 Days!

In this example, a video series offering training on how to create an online course is useful for course creators who want to offer their expertise as an added service, for online marketing coaches, and for course hosting platforms.

## 14. Challenge

By inviting your audience to join you and others to accomplish a goal, a challenge provides them with the chance to experience what it's like to work with you and what type of results they can expect.

**Example:** Ready to Thrive in Just 10 Minutes a Day? Join the Empowering 5-Day Challenge to Get You Feeling Your Best!

This example would work well for businesses in the fitness or health space. The challenge offers a sense of community and is a dynamic way to give your audience the chance to get to know you.

## Modify the Ideas To Fit Your Business and Industry

Use any of the ideas here to help you create your first lead magnet. Think about your audience and the problems you are solving for them. Then think of how you can dissect your solution into a small offering that has value for them. The offering needs to have enough information to give them something to work with right away while at the same time leaving them wanting more from you.

# Chapter 6 Questions/Exercises

1. What problem are you trying to solve?

_____
_____
_____
_____

2. What solution do you have to help your audience?

_____
_____
_____
_____

3. Can you give your solution out for free? Why or why not?

_____
_____
_____
_____

A note on freebies: Just because you have a free offer doesn't mean your target audience will opt-in to get it. You have to truly understand what they want and what their problem is. The Freebie Worksheet of the Launch Plan Worksheets will help you work through what a great freebie would be for your target audience. The Launch Plan Worksheets are available at digitalpixie.ca/worksheets. Enter code "MochaLatte" to get 35% off the regular price.

# Chapter 7: Guide to Landing Pages

## What Is a Landing Page and What Is It Used For?

A landing page is a single web page that is used to transform web visitors into subscribers and customers. A landing page can be used to capture emails to generate leads and build your mailing list. It can also be used as a sales page to sell your products or services. You can even use it to nurture relationships. In the simplest terms, a landing page is the page you drive web visitors to. Technically speaking, the homepage of your website can be called a landing page. However, in the world of sales funnels, when we refer to a landing page, we are usually referring to one page that has a very specific call-to-action (CTA).

A landing page (see example below) can be a stand-alone page that is separate from your website, but it can also be created as a page on your website. You can use a tool or platform that specializes in creating landing pages, or you can use your website to build your landing page. In Chapter 8, we'll take a look at the different types of landing pages along with a visual example of each type.

Sometimes it is better to build a dedicated page that is separate from your website, which can be done by using a dedicated landing page platform. Most of these platforms require no coding, which makes it easy for anyone to build a landing page.

There are several great reasons you may want to use a dedicated landing page platform:

1. You don't need to have a website. If you're just starting out and want to build up your mailing list for when you do have something to offer, you can create a landing page without having an existing site.

2. Your website might not have a builder or content management system that is flexible enough to create beautiful and converting landing pages. By using a platform that specializes in creating landing pages, you don't have to worry about figuring out how to do this on your website.

3. Your landing page has only one job to do, and that is to convert your audience. On a regular website, there is a navigation menu, your blog feed, your footer with social media icons, and your regular pop-up form. These distractions may cause people to leave your landing page before they sign up, which you want to avoid. Not having anything else on the page to distract your visitor invariably leads to better conversions.

If you use a third-party platform that's separate from your website, you can link to your landing page from your website. That way, you can seamlessly guide website visitors to your landing page, without them even knowing that they're technically leaving your website. This can be done by adding a menu item to your navigation menu that links to the landing page, or if the landing page platform has an integration capability with your website, you can integrate the two platforms together (you'll have to follow the instructions they provide). Integrating two platforms refers to connecting or combining the functionalities and data of two separate software systems or platforms to work together seamlessly. This integration allows for the exchange of information, automation of processes, and synchronization of data between the two platforms.

If you choose to keep everything under one roof and build your landing page on your website, I will suggest that you remove your regular menu, header, and footer from the landing page (which may or may not be possible depending on what platform you are using for your website) to focus your visitors' attention on your lead magnet and the sign-up fields. To do this, you may have to seek the assistance of a web developer.

4. The templates provided in your chosen landing page platform

will have been tested for conversions. This takes the guesswork out of you having to design an effective landing page.

5. Page speed plays a huge role in conversion. On a desktop, it takes five to eight seconds for a web visitor to leave your page if they don't see what they think they should see (interesting fact: that's less than the attention span of a goldfish, which is nine seconds!). On a mobile device, it's even faster: between three to five seconds. A landing page built on a dedicated platform typically loads faster than a page on your site because it doesn't have to load in all of the many other pages and images of your site as well, all of which potentially slow your site speed.

6. Every page built on a dedicated landing page platform is considered a single page. This means that you can brand it separately from your regular website if you want your product, program or service to have its own distinct brand. However, it's important to note that brand recognition is important, so if you are branding your landing page separately from your regular website, you'll want to still be able to tie in the two brands together somehow.

On a dedicated platform, each page has a separate section for SEO, analytics (to add Google Analytics or Facebook pixel codes), social media, and favicon (the tiny image that shows up in the tab when it's open in your browser). If you were to build your landing page on your website, it would be hard (although not impossible) to brand it separately from your website. You also wouldn't be able to easily add Google Analytics or Facebook pixel codes to your individual landing page because these generally apply to the entire site. It is possible if your website is on WordPress, but it would require a plugin, or a separate page template, and then you have to apply that page template to the page you are building. That all sounds complex even to me! My moto is: why make things harder for yourself? You have enough to worry about!

7. According to Leadpages (a top landing page builder), "Landing pages (built on a dedicated platform) have conversion rates that are two to ten times higher than the average webpage". This higher conversion rate is again due to landing pages having a single goal, which is to get your web visitors to take action. Landing pages are tailored to the specific goal and focus solely on the action you want your visitors to take. This takes me back to #3 above - fewer distractions lead to better conversion.

There are certain times when landing pages built on your own site will make more sense. This really depends on your strategy and overall goal. For example, if you are an e-commerce business and are launching a new product, it makes perfect sense to keep your landing page on your site. You can also do an A/B test (see Chapter 16) and have one on your site and one on a dedicated platform to see which one performs better.

## A Landing Page vs. a Website

When do you use a landing page and when do you use a website? A sales funnel landing page is meant for a single call-to-action; it is focused on one goal. A website is a collection of different pages.

While a website also focuses on the goal of getting more customers, it usually has different calls-to-action such as phone, email, complete a form, request a quote, etc. It is not necessary to have a call-to-action on every single page (although if you ask me, every website page should have a call-to-action, but that's a topic for another day). Some web pages also exist as an information hub and are not laser-focused on a single CTA.

## Must-Have Elements of a Landing Page

A great landing page is structured to show visitors (your leads) who you are, what you do, and why your offer is so awesome that they should opt-in or sign up right away. There's a science to landing pages. The following elements—all of which focus on a call-to-action and conversion—must be present to ensure success.

You can see how these elements are put together in the optional Launch Plan Worksheets available for purchase at digitalpixie.ca/worksheets (use the code "MochaLatte" to get it for $17).

## 1. Attention-Grabbing Headline

You need a clear and compelling headline that instantly communicates the purpose of the landing page and captures the visitor's attention. This headline should match what your visitors clicked on to get to your landing page (i.e. your Facebook ad, blog, or wherever else you're driving traffic from). This is your Unique Value Proposition (UVP) - a short summary of what your landing page is about. For example, "The Ultimate Guide to Walking Your Dog with Ease."

## 2. Supporting Subheadline

You can include a subheading to provide any additional information that supports your main headline and the content. For example: "Don't Lose Control: Discover the step-by-step process to walking your dog comfortably and confidently."

## 3. Your Offer

The success of your landing page will depend on how well you position and communicate your offer. The offer should consist of all or a combination of:

- An introduction to your offer

- Features and benefits
- Ideal audience that your offer is intended for
- Discount, bonuses or other limited-time promotions

## 3. Visual Appeal and Branding

Visuals set the scene and provide a unique user experience. A combination of your logo, hero (main) image, icons, other images, videos, colors, and fonts can convey a powerful story. Just as branding for your business is essential, so is the branding you use on your landing page. Keep your landing page clean, clear, and consistent to optimize and maximize conversions.

**Imagery**. Imagery is part of the visual appeal. Use a high-quality image (a low quality, blurry image is a turn-off) with a wow factor. You can purchase some great quality photos from photo banks such as iStock, Bigstock, Veer, Fotolia, or Adobe, to name a few. Unsplash, Pixabay, and Pexels are also great resources for stock photos that are free to use; however, keep in mind that many of the free photos available have already been used by other businesses and websites, so your audience may have seen the same photos elsewhere.

If you're a public figure and you yourself are your brand, don't be shy: use a great photo of yourself! (But, please, no selfies). If you don't have a professional headshot, it's probably time that you hire a photographer and get some professional quality photos that you can use for your landing page and all of your marketing.

Think of it this way: if you are representing your brand, what does your photo say about you and your business?

**Videos**. Although having a video on your landing page is not a must-have, stats show that landing pages with videos can increase conversions by 86%[1]. Since the majority of consumers (90%) prefer video content, smart marketers are working video into their landing pages more and more.

**Visual Breaks and Formatting.** Use bullet points, subheadings, images, and other visual elements to break up the text and make the page easier to read and more engaging.

**Responsive Design**. Ensure that the landing page is optimized for various devices, including desktops, tablets, and smartphones. There's nothing worse than landing on a page using your mobile device and the formatting is all off, or you can't really read the content. By optimizing your page for various devices, the likelihood of visitors staying on your page and converting increases exponentially.

## 4. Credibility - Social Proof

Social proof strengthens your Unique Value Proposition (UVP) and your credibility. This can be in the form of testimonials or reviews,

---

1 https://blog.wishpond.com/post/87901107699/what-are-the-benefits-of-video-on-landing-pages

awards, and public relations (media mentions). While including social proof is not always necessary, especially for a splash page or short squeeze page (refer to the chapter on Types of Landing Pages to learn about splash and squeeze pages), having social proof on your landing page increases the trust factor and may persuade your web visitors to take action.

## 5. Cost

The cost is an important element to have on your landing page. People don't want to sign up for anything or give up their information without knowing how much your offer is. If you're offering something for free, you should definitely make that fact visible. People love free stuff!

On a sales page, it's important to be transparent about the cost of your product or service.

## 6. About

People want to know who you (or your company) are and what makes you credible. Why are you offering this information? What is your experience? Whom do you serve? The "About" section on your website isn't always necessary to include on a landing page. Whether you should include one will depend on what type of landing page it is and what you are offering.

## 7. Opt-In Form

The opt-in form is the email capture. This is where you collect your lead's name and email address. If the landing page is a sales page, you won't have an opt-in form; instead, you'll have a checkout or cart section.

## 8. Call-To-Action

Your call-to-action (CTA) is where you capture your leads. This is where the conversion takes place. What do you want people to do? Buy now? Register for an event? Sign up for a webinar? Download a PDF? Your CTA asks your visitors to take action and should be crystal clear. You have to make it easy for your visitors to understand what you're asking them to do. Without a CTA, there is no conversion.

## 9. Checkout / Cart

A checkout or cart is only necessary on a sales page where you are selling something. If the landing page's intention is not to sell and your call-to-action is to opt-in, then you don't need to capture payment.

## 10. Countdown Timer or Scarcity Elements

A countdown timer is not a must-have element, but if there's a time-sensitive offer or limited availability, a countdown timer or other scarcity elements can create a sense of urgency, which can boost conversion.

## 11. Frequently Asked Questions

Having an FAQ section is highly recommended for sales pages. You want to anticipate questions that might deter or delay visitors from making that purchase by addressing them directly on the page.

# Chapter 7 Questions/Exercises

1. Which do you need right now - a website or a landing page?

2. What do you plan to offer or sell?

3. Why would people buy from you?

# Chapter 8: Types of Landing Pages

There are several types of landing pages, but for the purpose of building a funnel, we'll focus on two main types. It's important to know the difference so you can determine which type of landing page is best to use. If you're just starting out and only building your list at this time, you might use one type only. If you're a more seasoned business, eventually you might end up using more than one type of landing page.

## Splash Page

A splash page is a stand-alone page or pop-up that is used to deliver information such as an upcoming event or promotion before visitors enter your website. In the case of a funnel, when we refer to a splash page, we are referring to a page or pop-up that has an opt-in (email capture). Visitors have the option to opt-in or not, and they can still access the website content they originally intended to visit.

A splash page is short and meant to collect leads before visitors browse your website. The elements of a splash opt-in page are:

- Logo and branding (optional since a splash page is usually a part of your website)
- Attention-grabbing headline
- Supporting subheadline (optional)
- Brief description (optional)
- Captivating image/video
- Cost
- Form with a call-to-action (email capture)
- Exit option

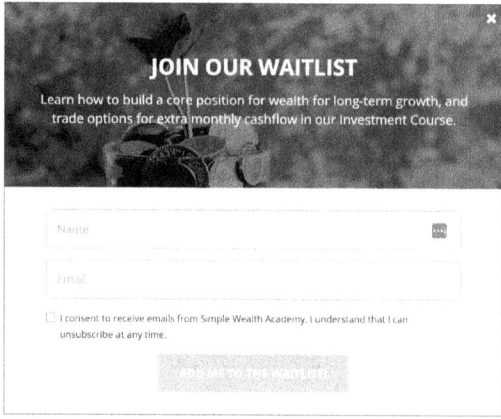

Sample Splash Page (Pop-Up Form)

# Squeeze Page

A squeeze page is a stand-alone page with an offer (free or paid) whose content can vary in length. It can be as short as a splash page, but the difference is that visitors arrive on this page specifically for the offer, not to browse your website. It is done as a landing page, not a pop-up.

A webinar landing page, for example, is a squeeze page. Elements of a squeeze page include:

- Logo and branding
- Attention-grabbing headline
- Supporting subheadline (optional)
- Brief description/introduction
- Your offer (optional benefits, features, audience)
- Cost
- Visuals (images, videos)
- About you/your company
- Social proof (optional)
- For webinars: date and time
- Call-to-action

## How Long Should Your Squeeze Page Be?

Whether your squeeze page is as short as a splash page or longer with benefits, features, audience, and social proof depends on your target audience and your traffic source.

If your audience already knows your brand and knows what to expect when they land on your squeeze page, a short one is probably sufficient. But if your audience needs a little more convincing, then you'll want to include more information.

Where and how you are driving traffic to your squeeze page also matters. If you have a longer ad explaining your offer, the squeeze page can be simple and short as your visitors already know what they'll be signing up for. If your ad is shorter, your audience will want to learn more about your offer, and this is where the additional information becomes extremely important.

Sample Squeeze Page (built on a dedicated landing page platform)

Types of Landing Pages - 75

# Sales Page

A sales page, also sometimes known as a sales letter, is used to generate sales. Instead of generating leads like a splash or squeeze page, a sales page focuses on revenue generation. It is a longer landing page and goes through, in detail, the offer, features, and benefits. It explains what the product or service is and typically includes social proof.

Elements of a sales page include:

- Logo and branding
- Compelling headline
- Supporting subheadline
- Your offer - intro, features, benefits, who it's for
- Visuals (images, videos)
- About you/your company
- Social proof
- Cost/investment
- Frequently Asked Questions
- Call-to-action
- Checkout cart / payment capture

On a sales page, as your goal is to capture your target audience's emotions, your sales copy is extremely important. It has to create a sense of connection between your audience and your offer. It has to uncover your audience's pain points and illustrate to your audience that your offer is the solution to their pain.

If writing is not your strength, work with a copywriter who specializes in sales pages.

Tip: refer to the end of this guide, which contains a list of resources with contacts for copywriters I personally recommend.

Sample Sales Page
(built on a website but can easily be done on a dedicated landing page platform)

# Chapter 8 Questions/Exercises

1. Which one do you think you'll need - a splash page or a squeeze page?

_____
_____
_____
_____

2. What do you want people to do once they land on your landing page?

_____
_____
_____
_____

When you're ready to see how to create your own splash, squeeze, and sales pages, go to digitalpixie.ca/worksheets and enter code "MochaLatte" at checkout.

# Chapter 9: Landing Page Copy

I'm sure you've heard it before that content is everything. And not just any content, but well-written content. Creating a landing page means that you need content (also called copy) to tell your audience what your landing page is about. Your landing page copy is not only an important part of your landing page; in fact, it could be argued that it is THE most important factor. You can have beautiful imagery and colors, but if your copy is insufficient, uninspiring, or gawky/poorly written, your chances of converting will decrease by a lot.

Your copy must be tight, relevant, and resonant. It should be engaging and full-voiced but also lean and clean.

When creating your landing page, keep in mind that the most

compelling information you include needs to be above the fold, which is the section of your site that viewers/visitors see without having to scroll down. What people see above the fold will determine whether they leave or stay on your page and then scroll down to see more. Anything below that, which typically requires you to scroll down, is considered to be *below the fold* and is secondary to the details above the fold.

## Attention-Grabbing Headline (and Subheadline)

Your headline is the first thing your visitors see and must be placed above the fold. It has to be attention-grabbing and emotionally accessible. What about your headline makes your visitors want to learn more? Remember, you have five to eight seconds to convince your audience to stay on your page (or only three to five seconds if they are on a mobile device). Hook them in with your headline!

## Your Offer

People's buying behavior is connected to their emotions. Studies have shown that 70% of people make emotionally driven purchases[1]. That's why it's important to make them feel. Whether they buy your offer will be highly dependent on your ability to connect with them on an emotional level. Your copy has to reflect your understanding of their

---

1 https://www.gallup.com/workplace/398954/customer-brand-preference-decisions-gallup-principle.aspx

pain points and provide reassurance that you can help them and that your offer is the exact thing to provide them relief.

Include the following as part of your offer:

**Introduction.** The introduction section is where you provide a short description of your offer.

**Features**. What's included in your offer and the value it provides to your audience relative to the cost of your offer? People always think about value. They might not need ALL the features, but the more perceived value in your offer there is, the higher the likelihood of conversion.

**Benefits.** How your offer benefits your audience and solves their pain points. What will happen if they don't buy your offer now?

**Audience.** Who or what kind of person your offer serves and why. Explanation of why they are experiencing the problem you are trying to solve.

**Discounts / Bonuses / Limited-Time Offers.** If your offer is time-sensitive or has limited availability, make this clear on the landing page. Offering a discount, bonus, or other limited-time offer can create a sense of scarcity and urgency.

**Call-To-Action.** Yes, copywriting matters in your CTA as well. A simple "sign up" or "subscribe" isn't going to cut it. Use your CTA to reassure your audience that they want or need your offer. For example,

"Yes, show me how to eat healthier!" is going to be more compelling than "sign up."

## Leave It To the Pros!

If copywriting isn't your jam, leave it to the pros and hire a professional copywriter who has experience with landing pages. If you don't pay for anything else, pay for copywriting! I recommend a few copywriters in the Resources section of this guide I have worked with personally. Don't underestimate the power of your landing page content. Having great copy that converts is essential to the success (or lack thereof) of your landing page.

# Chapter 9 Questions/Exercises

1. Who is your target audience you'll be speaking to on your landing page?

_____
_____
_____
_____

2. What type of emotion do you want to convey on your landing page?

_____
_____
_____
_____

In the Launch Plan Worksheets, you'll get sheets that guide you through creating each type of landing page to help you understand who you are/your business is, what you do, who your ideal client is, and why your visitors should take action on your landing page. Get the worksheets at digitalpixie.ca/worksheets and use code "MochaLatte" to receive your discount.

# Chapter 10: Comparison: Landing Page Platforms

There are many options available for creating your landing pages. If you already have a website, you can always make one there. You'll want to remove all distractions from your landing page as we touched on in Chapter 7.

If you:

a. Don't already have a website

b. Have one but can't easily create a landing page on it

c. Don't have the ability to remove the distractions from your web page that you'd use as a landing page

then you might want to consider a platform that specializes in landing pages. Chapter 12 compares different email marketing tools, some of which include the ability to create landing pages, giving you a 2-in-1 option, which may be more convenient than using separate platforms, one for email marketing and another for landing pages.

Something to consider is that specialized landing page platforms have tested their templates for maximum conversion. You can still create your own that will also convert, so don't let this be your deciding factor. In this chapter, we'll compare four popular landing page platforms.

Tip: new platforms are constantly coming out, and existing ones are continuously updated, so feel free to expand your research and review some of the other tools available on the market.

For a stand-alone landing page, my preference is Leadpages because it is cost effective, easy to use, and it has most of the features you need when you're just starting out. If you don't already have a website, you can even create a website using Leadpages.

Disclaimer: I'm an affiliate of different landing page platforms including Leadpages and some of the other ones mentioned throughout this book. Please use my link in the Resources section to try Leadpages for free for 14 days or scan the QR code here.

# Deciding On a Landing Page Platform: What To Consider

Before we dive into the pros and cons of each landing page platform, let's go over some of the basics you might want to consider.

## Budget

There's a wide range of pricing across the various platforms and many different plans to choose from. Some platforms offer a free option, but free plans always have limitations, such as the inability to connect to a custom domain. The free plan may be fine when you're first starting out, but it's not sustainable or recommended in the long run as your business grows. When you're ready to move into a paid plan, all platforms offer a monthly subscription and most offer annual billing, which may offer a slight discount over paying monthly.

## Templates

Does the platform offer templates for you to use or at least to start with that you can easily customize? Starting with a template and then customizing it to match your branding makes building your landing page easier, especially if you're not a trained graphic designer. Or if website design comes easily to you, perhaps templates aren't as important.

## Editor

What type of text editor does it have? Does it come with an easy drag-and-drop editor? Are the sections fixed (with very little flexibility to move elements around), or does it come with what's called a Canvas Editor, where you can drop your elements anywhere on the page, giving you full control of the design? If website design is not your forté, it might be an advantage for you to have fixed sections, which will give you predetermined design options. If you are a website designer, the lack of flexibility with fixed sections might be frustrating for you, and a platform with a Canvas Editor may be the better option.

## A/B Testing and Analytics

Does the platform have A/B testing capabilities? Does it have robust analytics so you can analyze the performance of your campaigns? (You will learn more about A/B testing in Chapter 16, including what it is and what to test). Not all platforms offer this feature, so you'll have to decide whether this option is important to you.

## Payment and Checkout

Some landing page platforms include payment and checkout capability, making it possible for you to sell your products and services right in the platform. Some don't include this feature but can be integrated with PayPal, Stripe, or both, while others don't offer this feature at all as they simply focus on creating landing pages with the idea that you would link the sale button to your own checkout platform. If you are selling a product or a service, you'll need to know where and how you'll be taking payment, and whether or not having an integrated checkout feature is important to you.

## Ability to Calculate Sales Tax

If you decide that having a checkout feature right in the platform is important, do you need it to be able to calculate sales tax? Sales tax is something to consider regardless of where you're taking payment. If as a business you need to charge sales tax, this feature is important to have as part of the checkout function.

## Email Marketing and SMS

Some landing page platforms include either email marketing or an SMS feature or both. Having an email marketing or SMS feature included with the landing page platform means you don't have to worry about integrating it with an external email marketing and/or SMS platform.

## Your Requirements

The requirements you have might be different from someone else's. It's important to understand what you need and also what you want but can live without in consideration of your overall budget for the platform. Now, let's go ahead and review the pros and cons of each landing page platform.

# Pros and Cons

## Leadpages

| Pros | Cons |
|---|---|
| • Affordability: $<br>• Leadpages is the most cost effective platform of the four reviewed<br>• Easy to use drag-and-drop editor<br>• 100+ templates<br>• Offers A/B testing<br>• Offers direct SMS integration<br>• Built-in checkout that integrates with both PayPal and Stripe<br>• Can be used to create a website in addition to landing pages<br>• Includes features for lead generation, such as pop-up forms and alert bars | • Limited customization: Extensive customizing of templates is challenging, and users with very specific design requirements may find the platform limiting |

## Instapage

| Pros | Cons |
|---|---|
| • Has canvas (blank) editor offering free-form drag-and-drop capability<br>• Has separate optimization for mobile devices<br>• Built-in checkout that integrates | • Affordability: $$$<br>• Traffic limitations: Depending on your subscription plan, Instapage may have limitations on the amount of traffic your landing pages can handle, |

| Pros | Cons |
|---|---|
| with PayPal<br>• Robust A/B testing features | • which may not be suitable for high-traffic campaigns<br>• A canvas editor can make customizing and building landing pages more challenging, for users whose design skills are lacking<br>• No direct SMS integration (must be set up via Zapier)<br>• No direct integration with Stripe (must be set up via Zapier) |

## Wishpond

| Pros | Cons |
|---|---|
| • Affordability: $<br>• Canvas editor allows free-form drag-and-drop page building<br>• Includes email automation<br>• Can upgrade to include email campaigns<br>• Offers direct SMS integration<br>• Built-in checkout that integrates with Stripe<br>• Social media tools for running contests and promotions on platforms like Facebook and Instagram to help boost social engagement | • A canvas editor can make customizing and building landing pages more challenging, for users whose design skills are lacking<br>• No integration with PayPal |

# Unbounce

| Pros | Cons |
|---|---|
| • Easy to use drag-and-drop editor<br>• Supports dynamic text replacement, allowing you to personalize landing page content based on the ad or keyword that brought the visitor to the page<br>• Secure - has SSL encryption for all landing pages<br>• Robust A/B testing features<br>• 100+ templates<br>• Has a sticky bar feature | • Affordability: $$<br>• The selection of templates is not as extensive as competitors' selections<br>• Customizing the templates is time consuming<br>• No direct SMS integration (must be set up via Zapier)<br>• No direct integration with PayPal and Stripe (must be set up via a third party) |

# Comparison Table

| Features & Benefits | Leadpages | Instapage | Wishpond | Unbounce |
|---|---|---|---|---|
| Price (USD) | Starts at $49/month | Starts at $299/month | Starts at $49/month | Starts at $99/month |
| Blank Template | ✓ | ✓ | ✓ | ✓ |
| Templates | ✓ | ✓ | ✓ | ✓ |
| Save Template or Add to Library | ✓ | ✓ | ✓ | No, but can download to save |
| Drag-and-Drop Editor | ✓ | ✓ Canvas editor | ✓ Canvas editor | ✓ |
| Custom Domain | ✓ | ✓ | ✓ | ✓ |
| Pop-Up Opt-In | ✓ | ✓ | ✓ | ✓ |
| Emails | Integrate with third party | Integrate with third party | Automation included. Campaigns on premium plan. | Integrate with third party |
| SMS | ✓ | Via Zapier | ✓ | Via Zapier |
| Checkout | ✓ | ✓ | ✓ | Via Checkoutpage.co |
| PayPal Integration | ✓ | ✓ | No | Via PayPal app |
| Stripe Integration | ✓ | Via Zapier | ✓ | Via Checkoutpage.co |
| A/B Testing | ✓ | ✓ | ✓ | ✓ |
| Analytics | ✓ | ✓ | ✓ | ✓ |
| Special Features | | Mobile optimization. Flexible editor. | Mobile optimization. Flexible editor. Publish anywhere. | Sticky bar |
| Sign Up | [QR] | [QR] | [QR] | [QR] |

# Chapter 10 Questions/Exercises

1. After looking through the pros and cons of each landing page platform, what features are most important for you?

2. If you have a product or service you plan to sell using a sales page, how are you going to take payment?

3. Which payment processor will you be using (for example, PayPal or Stripe)?

# Chapter 11: Nurture Emails: What, Why, How, and When?

## What Are Nurture Emails?

Email marketing is an effective and low cost way to market to your leads and existing customers. Nurture emails take email marketing to a higher level. They are different from the regular newsletter you might send out once a month. The purpose of nurture emails is to move your customers through your funnel, from the top to the bottom (where the conversion happens) through a series of emails. This is also known as a drip campaign (as in you're dripping the emails out one by one through the funnel) or email sequence (a sequence or series of emails).

## Why Do You Need Nurture Emails?

As mentioned above, nurture emails help you move leads through your funnel to turn them into paying customers. On average, research shows it takes about six to eight touch points[1] or contacts with you/your business to turn a lead into a paying client. Nurture emails help with those touch points.

But there's a strategy to nurture emails. As the name suggests, nurture emails are meant to "nurture" your cold leads to help them get to know you, your brand, and your offering, warming them up along the way.

## How: Copywriting Tips

Copywriting is the most important part of nurture emails. The overall ideas, language, and tone you use will make or break your emails' efficacy. The following tips will help you write your email copy. (To get specific help with copy you can use in your nurture emails, refer to the Nurture Emails Worksheet and Template in the Launch Plan Worksheets (at digitalpixie.ca/worksheets)).

1. Have an enticing subject line
2. Make it about them: use "you" not "I" or "we"
3. Show them how you understand their challenge or pain points

---

[1] https://www.salesforce.com/blog/takes-6-8-touches-generate-viable-sales-lead-heres-why-gp/
https://blog.hubspot.com/sales/the-ultimate-guide-to-prospecting-how-many-touchpoints-when-and-what-type
https://www.rainsalestraining.com/sales-research/sales-prospecting-research

4. Build credibility and trust
5. Show them how you can provide a solution to their challenge

# How: Structure

Each email should follow the same structure:

1. Subject line
2. Introduction
3. Body
4. Conclusion

Nurture emails are sent in a group of several emails known as email sequence. The idea is to send enough emails to get your message across, gain trust, and warm them up enough to convert to paying customers. In an email sequence, you can have a set of three, five, seven, ten, or even more nurture emails. How many you should send depends on your audience, overall goal, and strategy.

## Structure: Types of Subject Lines

We are bombarded with emails on a daily basis. Think about your own situation. How many emails do you get in a day? Do you open them all? Which emails do you open and why? Whether your readers open your email or not is dependent heavily on your subject line, so make it enticing enough for them to want to open your email. Think about what can make your email stand out in a busy inbox.

The following are different types of subject lines you can try:

**Urgency.** Example "Don't Miss Out! 50% OFF - Limited Time Offer - Only For The Next 24 Hours!"

**Educate.** Example: "Unlock the Secrets to a Powerhouse Website: 5 Must-Have Elements to Skyrocket Your Conversions!"

**Curiosity.** Examples: "Do You Know Why Your Diet Never Works? Unlock the 3 Reasons Your Diet Fails and How to Fix It!" or "How Josh lost 20lbs in one month using my 30-day meal plan".

**Question.** Example "Would you like to put an end to doggie drama? Unleash a bite-free future for your furry friend!"

**Personal connection.** One way to achieve a personal connection is by using the lead's first name. Another is to find a way to relate to them. Examples:

"Jane, what do you think of my latest recipe?"

"Jane, I couldn't figure out why my cucumber plants didn't produce cucumbers"

"Jane, guess who I ran into the other day?"

Of course, the subject (recipe, cucumbers, or someone you ran into) has to be something that relates to your readers that they can personally connect to.

**Story.** Examples: "I just ran into an old friend and guess what we talked about?" or "My client, Jenny, had to walk her dog at 4 a.m.!"

**About them.** Example: "Unlock the Secret to Skyrocket Your Client Base with this Proven Method!"

## Structure: Introduction

Just like any news article or press release, the first sentence in an email (after the headline/subject) needs to capture your readers' attention right away and give the reader what they're expecting (from the opt-in and your subject line).

The introduction sums up the reason for your email. Getting them to open your email is half the battle. The next half is getting them to actually READ it.

Personalizing your email by using your reader's first name is a good idea (i.e. Hello, Jane). When you personalize the email using their first name, you create a connection with them, making them more apt to continue reading.

Tip: when you are setting up your landing page capture fields, in addition to asking for the visitor's email address, include a field for your visitor to enter their first name. That will make it possible for you to personalize your emails to them later.

Here are a few examples of an introduction:

1. Are you tired of riding the diet roller coaster, going up and down like a yo-yo, and still not reaching your dream weight? You're not alone! It's time to unveil the secrets behind why

those diets never seem to stick around for good. Get ready to discover the top three reasons that have been silently sabotaging your efforts and learn how to finally achieve the lasting change you've been longing for!

2. Congratulations on your new website! Picture this: a converting website is like a well-crafted symphony, blending five essential elements in perfect harmony. But hold on, don't lean back and anticipate the melody to unfold effortlessly on its own! You might be missing out on some key notes, preventing your website from achieving its full musical potential.

3. A big flavorful "Thank You" for jumping aboard the culinary adventure with me in my sizzling webinar: "How to Prep Meals Like a Pro"! Did you miss any crucial tips or savor-worthy tricks during the live event? Fear not! I've got you covered. The replay of our culinary masterpiece is now ready for you to indulge in.

## Structure: Body

Congratulations, you've captured your readers' attention through your subject line and your introduction. Now they are at the body of your email, which is where you will continue to engage them. How relevant and engaging your email is will determine whether they keep reading or press "delete."

Remember that the goal is for you to gain their trust so they will want to hire you, buy your products, sign up for your course, etc. With that in mind, you want to make this email about them by providing them with information and/or resources that will help them solve their problem.

Here are some of the things you can include in the body of your email:

- Link to one of your blogs and why (don't just direct them to your blog without telling them how they will benefit from reading it)
- A testimonial or case study
- A video: testimonial, explainer video of your service, a personal hello from you with a short story, or a sneak peek of your offering
- A story of how you helped someone in a similar situation as them
- Link to another resource that is not yours. You want to limit doing this because you should always aim to drive traffic back to your site first. That said, if there's a really great resource that you feel will help them, then you can consider giving them this resource. After all, you want your reader to know that you're there to help!

## Structure: Conclusion

The conclusion of an email in email marketing is the closing part of the email where you wrap up your message and encourage the reader to take a specific action. It serves as a call-to-action (CTA) and leaves a lasting impression on the reader. Writing an effective conclusion is crucial for increasing engagement and achieving your email marketing goals, whether it's promoting a product, driving traffic to your website, or encouraging subscribers to sign up for an event.

Here are some tips on how to write a compelling conclusion for an email in email marketing:

**Be clear and concise:** Keep your conclusion succinct and to the point. Avoid excessive wordiness and make sure your message is easily understood.

**Include a strong call-to-action (CTA):** Clearly state what action you want the recipient to take. This could be to visit a specific webpage, make a purchase, subscribe to a newsletter, or RSVP to an event. Use action-oriented language that creates a sense of urgency.

**Create a sense of value:** Let the recipient know how they will benefit from taking the desired action. Highlight the value of your offer or the benefits they'll receive.

**Personalize if possible:** If you have data on the recipient, use it to personalize the conclusion. Address them by their name and tailor the

CTA based on their preferences or past interactions.

**Express gratitude:** Show appreciation for the recipient's time and interest. A simple "Thank you" can go a long way in building a positive relationship with your audience.

**Use a friendly tone:** Keep the tone of the conclusion friendly and approachable. This helps build a connection with the reader.

Here are a couple of examples of a conclusion:

1. Jane, you're not alone in your struggle with your roller coaster of a diet. But now it's time to put an end to the cycle and reveal the secrets that have been sabotaging your success. Discover the top three reasons behind the setbacks, and take the first step towards achieving your dream weight with lasting change. Let's embark on this journey together and make your health and wellness a priority!

2. Congratulations once again on launching your new website! But don't sit back and wait for results to magically appear. Fine-tune your website to ensure it reaches its full potential by incorporating the five essential elements. Let's work together to make your website an exceptional success story!

## Structure: Putting It Together

Now that you have a better understanding of the structure of an email, let's put one together as an example. You can follow this format using the Email Marketing template included in the worksheet add-on.

| Subject: (story) | My client Jenny had to walk her dog at 4 a.m.! |
|---|---|
| Introduction: | Hello, [First Name], My client Jenny had to walk her dog at 4 a.m. because she needed to guarantee that she wouldn't run into any other dogs. |
| Body: (testimonial) | The problem? Jenny was tired from having to wake up before the sun rises just so she could walk her dog. It was starting to have a negative effect on her. She was beginning to resent her dog and was at her wits' end. When she came to me, she was in tears. She was so torn and heart broken. She loved her dog, but she was also on the brink of giving her away. After taking my Dog Training program, here's what she had to say: "insert testimonial" |
| Conclusion: | [Name], you don't have to be like Jenny. You don't have to walk your dog at 4 a.m., because my Dog Training program is now open. But there's only space for five participants and their dogs (so each person and their dog get my full attention), and it's first come first serve. I'm giving you first dibs because you downloaded my tips on how to walk your dog with ease. I know you downloaded that because you need help, and I promise I can help you. Here's the link to sign up for the program: [link] I hope to see you soon! [Your name] |

## How: Automate

You're definitely not expected to send each email individually and manually. You'll give up after the first day! Use an email marketing platform and automate the process. Work smarter, not harder!

## When Do You Send These Emails?

Nurture emails are meant to nurture your leads, so they typically go out after a lead magnet or webinar/event sign-up. But there are also emails that go out before, depending on which part of the funnel these emails are for.

**Pre-webinar/event emails** - these emails go out after your leads sign up for your webinar or event and before the webinar/event. They consist of a confirmation email that goes out immediately after registration and two to four reminder emails before the webinar/event. The reminder emails can go out 24-48 hours before the event, one hour before the event, and 10 or 15 minutes before the event. You might even want one that goes out right when the event starts. Keep in mind that free webinars/events have a higher rate of no-shows than paid ones, so you can take the opportunity to create excitement through these emails to increase your leads' chances of attending your event.

**Post-webinar/event emails** - these emails go out after your leads have attended your webinar or event. It's through these emails that you can nurture them to take action, whether that's to sign up for a consultation or to buy something from you. If you don't have anything to offer yet, you can use these emails to keep them interested so they continue to look forward to your regular newsletters. These emails can be anywhere from three to fifteen emails. If you are offering a free consultation, three to five emails might be sufficient. If these emails are meant to sell your service or product, you might need up to 15 emails. You can send these emails two to four days apart. However, if you have a limited-time offer; for example, your offer is only good for 24 hours after the webinar/event, you'll want to send several emails within 24 hours. This could be:

- Immediately after the webinar/event followed by
- 8 hours after the event
- 16 hours after the event
- 23 hours after the event for last call

**Post lead magnet sign-up** - these emails go out after your leads have signed up to receive your lead magnet. The purpose of these emails is the same as the post-webinar/event emails.

**Sales emails** - sales emails are exactly as they sound. They are meant to sell your product or service. The post-webinar/event sequence and post lead magnet sign-up sequence are considered sales emails if you have the intention of selling. If you have a cart closing date (which means that what you are selling will no longer be available for purchase after a certain date), you can also send several emails on the last day to create a sense of urgency. For example, for a cart that closes at 12 a.m. (midnight), the sequence could look like this:

- 2 days after the previous email followed by
- 5 hours after the previous email
- 5 hours after the previous email
- 8 hours after the previous email
- 2 hours after the previous email or 4 hours before the cart closes
- 3 hours after the previous email or 1 hour before the cart closes
- 15 minutes before cart closes for last call

**Abandoned cart emails** - these emails go out after your leads have gone all the way to checkout but did not complete the purchase, i.e. they have abandoned the cart. The purpose of these emails is to remind them that they almost made the purchase but didn't and to nudge them toward completing that purchase. You might want to consider offering an incentive such as a discount or a freebie with purchase. There are usually two to three emails in this sequence. The first email is usually sent 6-24 hours after, followed by 72 hours after, and optionally, one week after the cart was abandoned.

**Post-purchase emails** - these emails go out after your leads have turned into paying customers and made that purchase! This email sequence will consist of a confirmation email and details about their purchase. There are usually one to four emails in this sequence.

## Success Factors

Remember that the goal of your nurture emails is to convert your leads into paying customers. You want to sell to your leads without sounding too much like a salesperson because most people don't like being sold to. You want them to feel that they need your product or service and therefore they are making the decision to buy from you (and not that you're making that decision for them). Nurture emails can be very effective at doing this.

Keep in mind the following factors for maximum success:

1. Your emails need to be relevant. For example, you do not want to send emails to cat owners when you are selling dog-related products.

2. You need to provide a ton of value in your emails. This is a two-way street. You want to give your leads as much information as possible that will help them solve their current problem. By providing value in every email, you'll make them want to open and read your next emails. You can include one or more of the following (but never all in one email as that can be overwhelming):

- Video
- Link to one of your blogs (make sure it's a blog that is helpful for the situation they're in)
- Case studies
- Downloadable worksheets

3. Provide social proof. How have you helped other people? By providing social proof, your leads can start to envision what is possible for them.
4. Make it about them not about you. Help them feel seen and understood. This isn't about you making a sale; this is about you helping them. And by helping them, you make the sale.

# Chapter 11 Questions/Exercises

1. How are nurture emails different from sending out regular newsletters?

2. Name three factors that you can include in your nurture emails to ensure success.

3. When is the best time of day to send your nurture emails that you feel would get the most response from your audience?

Tip: Before you dive into developing your nurture sequence, make things easier for yourself by starting with an outline. After working through the Nurture Emails Worksheet from the Launch Plan Worksheets (at digitalpixie.ca/worksheets), you can use the email template to help you write your copy.

# Chapter 12: Comparison: Email Marketing Tools

There are many options for email marketing. In the following pages, I outline the pros and cons of some of the most popular email marketing platforms as well as include a quick birds-eye view comparison. Feel free to go beyond this list and review some of the other tools available. Note that these platforms are constantly updated and new updates may have been released since the publication of this book.

My favorite email marketing platform is MailerLite. It is very cost-effective, especially for someone just starting out, yet it offers a ton of options and almost everything you need for building your entire funnel. As a disclaimer, I am an affiliate of MailerLite and some of the other marketing platforms as well. As someone who specializes in setting up funnels, I work with a lot of platforms/ systems and know the ins and outs of many of them. To sign up for MailerLite and get 30 days of Pro for free, use the link in the Resources chapter of the book or scan the QR code here.

## Deciding On an Email Marketing Platform: What to Consider

To help decide which email marketing platform you should sign up for, we'll have a look at some of the basics to consider as you make your decision.

### Budget

Email marketing platforms come in a wide range of prices. Just like landing pages, some email marketing platforms offer a free plan with limitations. If your budget is small and you prefer to use a free plan, you'll have to decide if you can work within those limitations. The limitations can vary depending on the platform, but an example could be the lack of an automation function. If you feel you need the features available on the paid plans, you'll have to decide on the budget you're comfortable paying on a monthly or annual basis.

### Contact Management

Being able to segment your subscribers helps you send relevant emails to each of your segments. Sending relevant emails increases engagement, open rates, and click-through rates. When deciding on an email marketing platform, you'll want to review the platform's segmentation feature. Does it use different lists, or is it one list with multiple tags or groups within the list? Can you segment based on certain conditions; for example, those who purchased within the last six months, or those who purchased products A and C but didn't purchase product B?

## Email Automation

Automations allow you to send timely emails based on predefined triggers or schedules. They're also used to create drip campaigns, welcome sequences, or any other emails based on specific actions. The point of having an email marketing platform is instead of using an email service such as Gmail, you can automate your email workflows. When reviewing the platforms, learn how their email automation works and whether or not it will meet your needs.

## Templates

Does the platform offer templates for you to use, or at least to start with, that you can easily customize? Starting with a template and then customizing it to meet your needs will make creating an email marketing template easier, especially if design isn't your strongest skill.

## Design Options and Editor

What type of editor does the email marketing platform have? Does it have an easy drag-and-drop editor, or does it have more of a text editor (think Microsoft Word or Google Docs)? Do you want to send out pretty emails with images/graphics, or will you typically send text-based emails with few-to-no images? This depends on what your business is and whether you have the type of business that relies heavily on visuals such as e-commerce, or whether you have a service-based business that doesn't require as many visuals.

## A/B Testing and Analytics

Does the platform have A/B testing capabilities? Does it have robust analytics so you can analyze the performance of your email campaigns? Learn more about A/B testing in Chapter 16, including what it is and what to test. Not all platforms offer this feature, so you'll have to decide whether this is something you want as an option.

## Dynamic Content

In an email marketing platform, dynamic content refers to the ability to customize the content of an email based on various factors such as recipient demographics, behavior, preferences, or other data points. Instead of sending the same static email to every subscriber, dynamic content allows marketers to personalize the email content to make it more relevant and engaging for each recipient. For example, you can choose to show or hide a section in your email depending on whether or not the recipient has previously bought from you before. Is this an important feature for you to have? Can you live without this feature?

## Opt-In Forms

Your email marketing platform should have opt-in forms that allow you to collect subscribers. The one thing to consider is whether you can create multiple opt-in forms. Some platforms only allow one opt-in form, which limits your ability to create a separate form for each group or tag and which can be so helpful for segmentation. Another thing to consider is what you can do with the opt-in forms. Can you embed them somewhere else? Can you create pop-up forms?

## Landing Page Feature

Some email marketing platforms offer the ability to create landing pages, which is a great feature to have so you don't have to create your landing page using another platform. However, some platforms only offer landing pages for the purpose of collecting subscribers and don't give you the option to create landing pages without an opt-in form on them. This means that you would have to create your sales pages somewhere else, such as on your website or a stand-alone landing page platform. You can refer back to Chapter 7 for more information on landing pages.

## Integration and Compatibility

You may want to consider the compatibility of the email marketing platform with other tools and platforms such as CRM systems, e-commerce, social media, landing page platforms, and your website. Does it have access to API or integrations with third-party applications for seamless data exchange? Do you need it to integrate with a specific platform? For example, if you have an e-commerce business, you probably want an email marketing platform that can integrate with your e-commerce platform and segment your customers accordingly.

## Scalability and Pricing

If you start with the free plan or the lowest cost plan, are you able to upgrade easily when your business grows to accommodate your growing email list? Does the upgraded pricing seem reasonable to you from a cost perspective? The price might start really low and affordable, but as your business grows, it can become extremely expensive.

## Your Requirements

By evaluating these features, you can select an email marketing platform that best suits your business requirements and helps you achieve your marketing objectives effectively.

# Pros and Cons

## MailerLite

| Pros | Cons |
|---|---|
| • Affordability: $<br>• Intuitive and user-friendly<br>• Easy to use drag-and-drop editor<br>• Robust automation for the price<br>• A/B testing capability<br>• Includes landing page builder<br>• Includes website builder<br>• Dynamic content - you can show/hide content for certain groups<br>• Can create multiple forms (both embedded and pop-up) for the same group/audience<br>• Pop-up forms can be easily added to an external website such as WordPress<br>• You can show/hide pop-up forms on specific pages, which can help with conversion<br>• Can add polls and surveys directly in the email<br>• Has event RSVP capability<br>• Robust behavior settings - you can choose when you want to | • Text-only option is not automatic and has to be edited for every campaign, which can be annoying<br>• Landing page builder is great, but not as robust as other dedicated landing page platforms<br>• You can't move subscribers to start another automation at the end of an existing automation (it is possible using a workaround)<br>• No option for Facebook lead ads<br>• WooCommerce e-commerce integration can be a bit clunky<br>• 24/7 phone and chat support are only available on upgraded plans (email- only support for free plans) |

- show the pop-up, set frequency, sand adjust visibility settings
- E-commerce integration allows you to send campaigns and automations (integrates with Shopify) based on specific product purchases
- Upgraded plan offers promo pop-ups
- Upgraded plan offers auto-resend
- Upgraded plan offers customization on the unsubscribe page
- Upgraded plan offers the ability to send based on time zone

## MailChimp

| Pros | Cons |
|---|---|
| • Includes a landing page builder<br>• Easy to use drag-and-drop editor<br>• Includes a survey feature<br>• Upgraded plan offers the ability to send based on time zone | • Affordability: $$ - it can get pricey as your subscriber count increases<br>• Unsubscribers are counted in the total subscriber count, which can put you at the next level of pricing<br>• Multiple automations are not available in the free plan<br>• You can only create one form per audience, and there isn't an |

|  | - ability to create a form for tagged contacts. This makes it difficult to create different lead magnets
- No customization for the unsubscribe page. Subscribers can't choose to opt-out of certain lists because there's only one list (audience)
- No direct integration with Shopify (it requires a third-party app)
- There's a cap on the number of emails you can send per month, even on the highest plan
- No A/B testing capability |
|---|---|

## ConvertKit

| Pros | Cons |
|---|---|
| - No drag-and-drop visual editor. This can be viewed as an advantage for businesses who send emails with more text than imagery
- You can tag subscribers based on their link click activity for further segmentation
- Email sequences are set up separately from the visual | - Affordability: $$$
- Text-only email. This can be viewed as a disadvantage for businesses who want to or need to send visual-based emails
- Email sequences are set up separately from the visual automation, which can make it complicated for a less tech-savvy person |

| | |
|---|---|
| automation, which makes it possible to set up a more robust funnel<br>• Includes templated landing pages<br>• Includes templated forms<br>• Can create multiple forms, making it ideal for lead magnets<br>• A/B testing is available<br>• Has e-commerce integration | • Landing pages and forms are not as customizable as some of the other email marketing platforms<br>• No promo pop-ups<br>• No direct integration with Squarespace (must be embedded as a form)<br>• No dynamic content<br>• No customization for the unsubscribe page<br>• Can't create a landing page without a form as the main focus of ConvertKit is lead building and lead generation |

## ActiveCampaign

| Pros | Cons |
|---|---|
| • No drag-and-drop visual editor. This can be viewed as an advantage for businesses who send emails with more text than imagery<br>• Robust automation capability<br>• Advanced segmentation capability - you can segment subscribers based on their action, such as which pages they have viewed on your website | • Affordability: $$$$<br>• No pop-up forms<br>• No promo pop-ups<br>• No direct integration with Squarespace (must be embedded as a form)<br>• Text-only email. This can be viewed as a disadvantage for businesses who want to or need to send visual-based emails |

| | |
|---|---|
| • Has built-in CRM functionality<br>• You can create multiple forms<br>• Has landing pages<br>• Has dynamic content functionality<br>• Has robust e-commerce integration | • Higher learning curve because of the complexity of the platform |

# Comparison Tables

| Features & Benefits | MailerLite | MailChimp | ConvertKit | Active Campaign |
|---|---|---|---|---|
| Free Plan | Up to 1000 subscribers | Up to 500 subscribers | Up to 300 subscribers | No |
| Price (USD) Up to 1000 Up to 5000 Up to 10,000 Up to 25,000 | $21/month $39/month $87/month $159/month | $23/month $59/month $87/month $225/month | $29/month $79/month $119/month $199/month | Starts at $39/month $106.67/month $187.67/month $309.17/month |
| Monthly Email Sends | Unlimited | Up to 500,000 on highest plan | Unlimited | Unlimited |
| Subscriber Count | Counts only active, unique subscribers | Counts unsubscribes and duplicates | Counts total unique subscribers | Counts active, unique subscribers |
| List Management | One main list. Uses groups. | Up to one audience (list) in free plan. More in paid plans. | One main list. Uses tags. | Unlimited |
| Tag Management | No - uses groups | ✓ | ✓ | ✓ |
| Group Management | ✓ | ✓ | No - uses tags | No |
| Segmentation | ✓ | Limited | ✓ | ✓ |
| Automation | ✓ | Limited depending on plan | ✓ | ✓ |
| Multi-Entry Trigger | ✓ | No | ✓ | ✓ |
| File Attachment | No | ✓ | ✓ | No |
| Video Block | ✓ | ✓ | ✓ | ✓ |
| Pop-Up Forms | ✓ | ✓ One per audience | ✓ | ✓ |
| Embedded Forms | ✓ | ✓ | ✓ | ✓ |
| Promotion Pop-Up Forms | ✓ On paid plan | No | ✓ | No |
| Drag-and-Drop Editor | ✓ | ✓ | No | ✓ Limited options |

| Features & Benefits | MailerLite | MailChimp | ConvertKit | Active Campaign |
|---|---|---|---|---|
| Dynamic Content | ✓ | ✓ | No | ✓ |
| Unsubscribe Page Builder | ✓ | No | No | ✓ |
| A/B Testing | ✓ | No | ✓ | ✓ |
| Auto Resend | ✓ | No | No | No |
| Deliver by Time Zone | ✓ | No | No | No |
| Landing Pages | ✓ | ✓ | ✓ | ✓ |
| Custom Domains | Unlimited on paid plans | Limited | ✓ | ✓ On upgraded plans |
| RSS Campaigns | ✓ | No | ✓ | ✓ |
| Facebook Lead Ad | Via Zapier | ✓ | Via Zapier | ✓ |
| E-commerce Campaigns | ✓ | ✓ | ✓ | ✓ |
| E-commerce Integrations | Shopify WooComerce Sqsuarespace | Shopify - via Shopsync WooCommerce Squaresapce | Shopify WooCommerce Squarespace - via form embed | Shopify WooCommerce Squarespace - via form embed |
| Landing Page Integrations | All via Zapier: ClickFunnels Leadpages Instapage | ClickFunnels Leadpages Instapage | ClickFunnels Leadpages Instapage | ClickFunnels Leadpages Instapage |
| WordPress Integration | ✓ | ✓ | ✓ | ✓ |
| Payment Integration | Stripe | Stripe | Stripe | Stripe |
| Special features | Surveys & polls. Event RSVP | Surveys | Can tag link clicks | |
| Limitations | Text-only emails aren't automatic | Can't move from one list to another | Opt-in form on all landing pages | |
| Sign up | [QR code] | [QR code] | [QR code] | [QR code] |

| Features & Benefits | Constant Contact | Drip | AWeber | Brevo |
|---|---|---|---|---|
| Free Plan | ✓ Very limited features | No | 30-day free trial | ✓ Up to 300 emails |
| Price (USD) Up to 1000 Up to 5000 Up to 10,000 Up to 25,000 | $29/month $79month $119/month $199/month | $39/month $79/month $124/month $369/month | $29/month $49/month $69/month $149/month | Starts at $25/month for all, limited to 10,000 emails/month. Limited features. |
| Monthly Email Sends | Unlimited | Unlimited | Unlimited | 100,000 max on some plans |
| Subscriber Count | Counts total unique subscribers | Counts active subscribers | Counts unsubscribes and duplicates | Based on email limits |
| List Management | One main list - uses tags | One main list - uses tags | ✓ | ✓ |
| Tag Management | ✓ | ✓ | ✓ | ✓ |
| Group Management | No | ✓ | ✓ | ✓ |
| Segmentation | ✓ | ✓ | ✓ | ✓ |
| Automation | ✓ Sequence needed | ✓ | ✓ Limited | ✓ |
| Multi-Entry Trigger | No | ✓ | No | ✓ |
| File Attachment | ✓ | No | ✓ | ✓ |
| Video Block | ✓ | ✓ | ✓ | No, use image instead |
| Pop-Up Forms | ✓ | ✓ | No | ✓ |
| Embedded Forms | ✓ | ✓ | Limited | ✓ |
| Promotion Pop-Up Forms | ✓ | ✓ | No | No |
| Drag-and-Drop Editor | No | ✓ | ✓ | ✓ |
| Dynamic Content | ✓ | ✓ | ✓ | ✓ |
| Unsubscribe Page Builder | No | ✓ | No | No |

| Features & Benefits | Constant Contact | Drip | AWeber | Brevo |
|---|---|---|---|---|
| A/B Testing | ✓ | ✓ | ✓ | ✓ |
| Auto Resend | No, but can resend after | No | Via automation | No |
| Deliver by Time Zone | No | No | ✓ | No |
| Landing Pages | ✓ | No | ✓ | ✓ |
| Custom Domain | ✓ | ✓ | ✓ | ✓ |
| RSS Campaigns | ✓ | ✓ | ✓ | ✓ |
| Facebook Lead Ad | Via Zapier | ✓ | Via Zapier | Via Zapier |
| E-commerce Campaigns | No, use tags as a workaround | ✓ | ✓ | ✓ |
| E-commerce Integrations | Shopify WooComerce Squarespace - via form embed | Shopify WooComerce Squarespace - via Zapier | Shopify WooComerce Squarespace - via form embed | Shopify WooComerce Squarespace - via Zapier |
| Landing Page Integrations | ClickFunnels Leaadpages Instapage | ClickFunnels Leaadpages Instapage | ClickFunnels Leaadpages Instapage | All via Zapier: ClickFunnels Leaadpages Instapage |
| Wordpress Integration | ✓ | ✓ | ✓ | ✓ |
| Payment Integration | Stripe | Stripe | Stripe | Stripe |
| Special features | Can tag link clicks | | | All plans include unlimited contacts |
| Limitations | | | | |
| Sign Up | | | | |

# Chapter 12 Questions/Exercises

1. What do you look for in an email marketing platform?

2. Now that you've gone through the pros and cons of the different email platforms, which features do you feel are most important for you?

# Chapter 13: Online Courses

Online courses are programs that are offered virtually over the Internet. They have become very popular for a number of reasons:

1. Online courses enable individuals to learn from any location with an Internet connection. This flexibility is especially beneficial for those who cannot attend traditional in-person classes due to geographical constraints, work commitments, or other reasons.
2. Course materials can be accessed at any time, and they are usually digital.

Although some online courses have a set start and end date, many offer self-paced learning, allowing participants to establish their own schedules and progress through the material at their own speed.

Many businesses and entrepreneurs are opting to deliver their programs online for the following reasons:

1. You can help more people with an online course than you can one-on-one. For a live course, instead of coaching one client at a time, you can work with a small group and determine just how many participants you can handle before cutting off enrollment. For an on-demand course, you're able to serve an unlimited number of clients. They can even buy the course and take part in it while you're asleep or on vacation!

2. While online courses take more time on the front end to set up and build, once they are running, they demand less of your time than one-on-on programs. For example, for a weekly one-on-one program that's one hour long, you'll end up spending 20 hours per week for 20 clients. But with an online program, you would spend only one hour with however many people you've admitted into the group.

An online course can help you create passive income especially if you set it up as an on-demand course.

# Chapter 13 Questions/Exercises

1. Is creating an online course something that you want to do?

Y/N

2. If you answered yes to the above, why do you want to create an online course? If you answered no, why not?

_____
_____
_____

Head over to the "Creating Your Online Course Worksheet" on the Launch Plan Worksheets to help you plan and build your Online Course. The Launch Plan Worksheets are available at digitalpixie.ca/worksheets for only $17 (regular price $27) with the code "MochaLatte".

# Chapter 14: Comparison: Online Course Platforms

If you've decided to create an online course, you'll need a way to deliver the course to your clients. You can deliver your course simply by uploading videos to YouTube using the "Unlisted" option and send participants your course video links by email. This is a good option if you're just starting out because it's easy and free! The downside is your clients will need to keep their emails and search through them any time they want to find the course videos. It is also easy for them to share your course by forwarding the emails to others. (You can ask the participants nicely not to do this, and most people will be respectful, but it can easily happen).

Another option is to create a password-protected page on your website and house your course videos there. The disadvantage of doing this is that it uses a single password that all clients share. This again makes it easy for clients to share your password with others; plus, if you ever change the password, you will have to let all of your clients know.

The most favorable way to deliver your course is to use a specialized platform for online courses that requires your clients to log in and gives them the ability to track their progress as they move through the course. Once you have more than one course on offer, it might be time to consider a more sophisticated solution. There are many advantages to using online course platforms including the ability to bundle courses together and having a single space that makes it easy for your clients to view all the courses they have signed up for.

In the following pages, we'll compare six popular online course platforms including pros and cons of each. Feel free to go beyond this list and check out other platforms. A few of the platforms mentioned on the list are often considered "all-in-one" platforms because you can create landing pages, opt-in forms, email automation, and host your online courses on the same platform. Keep in mind that these platforms are constantly updated and some of these may have been updated since the publication of this guide.

# Deciding On an Online Course Platform: What To Consider

Before we dive into the pros and cons of each online course platform, let's take a look at some of the features.

## Budget

Just like your landing page and email marketing platform, you'll have to know your budget and what you are willing to spend on a course platform.

## Course Creation and Management

Does the platform allow video hosting, text, images, quizzes, and PDFs? Can it host videos or do you have to upload videos first to YouTube and then link from YouTube? Can you customize and organize your course structure, or are there limitations with the way you will have to organize your course?

## Ease of Use

How easy is the platform to use for you and also for your students? Is the interface intuitive? You want to make it as easy as possible for your students to find the information they're looking for, so it has to be organized in a user-friendly way. On the back end where you would create your course(s) and set up the admin, some platforms can be more difficult to use with a higher learning curve while some are fairly easy to figure out.

## Bundling Products

Bundling products refers to grouping multiple individual courses or products together into a single package or bundle for sale to customers. This bundling strategy offers several potential benefits including cost savings and convenience for your students, and cross-selling or upselling opportunities for your business. Not all platforms offer this feature, and the ones that do may only offer it in the higher paid plans.

## Customization of Course Landing Page

Every online course platform offers a landing page for each course. However, how much you can customize the landing page in terms of colors, branding, and ability to add or remove certain sections will differ across platforms.

## Payment

As a course creator, you'll probably want to offer pricing options such as one-time payment, payment plans over a number of months, or even a membership option. Check to see whether the course platform allows you to offer different pricing options. You'll also want to check what payment processor it integrates with, what the transaction fee is if any, and whether or not you can charge sales tax.

## Community and Membership

Are you planning to offer membership or have a community for your students? If you are, a membership or community feature within the platform itself might be advantageous. If it doesn't have this feature, you can always use an external membership platform.

## Your Needs

By considering these features, you can select an online course platform that aligns with your teaching style, course content, and business goals, ultimately providing a valuable learning experience for your students.

## Pros and Cons

### ClickFunnels

| Pros | Cons |
| --- | --- |
| • Has pre-built funnel templates for different purposes<br>• Separate mobile optimization<br>• Offers membership<br>• Includes basic email marketing on the upgraded plan<br>• Includes SMS capability<br>• Basic automation is available on the upgraded plan | • Affordability: $$<br>• Calculating sales tax requires a third-party app at an additional cost and is only available for U.S. customers<br>• Email marketing is very basic<br>• Automations feature is very basic<br>• Multi-currency is available |

| Pros | Cons |
|---|---|
| • Allows you to bundle courses<br>• Allows you to have unlimited products<br>• No transaction fees for product sales<br>• Scrapes information on customers and allows you to view customer details | through a third-party app at an additional cost |

## Kartra

| Pros | Cons |
|---|---|
| • Very robust<br>• Offers many different entry points<br>• Includes email marketing and email sequences<br>• Includes SMS capability<br>• Includes automations<br>• Includes landing pages<br>• Has sales funnel templates<br>• Allows you to bundle courses<br>• Includes a chat support functionality option to give you the ability to offer chat support to your clients<br>• Build and manage memberships<br>• Supports an unlimited number of products | • Affordability: $$<br>• Learning curve is high - it can be very complex to understand and set up<br>• The analytics are minimal and not as comprehensive as other platforms<br>• Limited third-party integrations |

|  |  |
|---|---|
| • Has the ability to calculate sales tax, which is a huge bonus<br>• Has the ability to offer multi-currency<br>• No transaction fees for product sales |  |

## Kajabi

| Pros | Cons |
|---|---|
| • Very simple to use<br>• Beautiful templates<br>• Can build a website on Kajabi including a blog<br>• Offers membership<br>• Includes landing pages<br>• Includes email marketing<br>• Includes email automation<br>• Includes membership<br>• Can bundle courses<br>• Has the ability to offer multi-currency | • Affordability: $$$<br>• For the website, no drop-down menus<br>• Courses are limited to three in the basic plan<br>• Email marketing and automation are not as robust as other platforms<br>• Can't calculate sales tax<br>• No SMS functionality (must use third-party platform) |

# Podia

| Pros | Cons |
|---|---|
| - Affordability: $<br>- Free plan available<br>- Very simple to use<br>- Includes basic landing pages for the purpose of list building<br>- Includes email marketing and automation on the upgraded plan<br>- Can calculate sales tax<br>- Can bundle courses<br>- Unlimited products on the paid plan (only one on the free plan)<br>- No transaction fees on paid plans | - Lack of customization<br>- Email marketing and automation are basic in comparison to other platforms<br>- Analytics aren't very robust in comparison to other platforms<br>- No SMS functionality (must use third-party platform)<br>- Transaction fee is high on the free plan<br>- Does not support multi-currency |

# Teachable

| Pros | Cons |
|---|---|
| - Affordability: $<br>- Free plan available<br>- Very simple to use<br>- Can bundle courses<br>- Unlimited products<br>- Can customize landing pages with HTML and CSS if you have knowledge of coding<br>- Has membership option | - Not an all-in-one (no email marketing, no landing pages except for the course sales pages)<br>- Automations available for the courses only<br>- Lack of customization<br>- Charges transaction fees<br>- Can't calculate and collect sales tax |

# Thinkific

| Pros | Cons |
|---|---|
| • Affordability: $<br>• Free plan available<br>• Very simple to use<br>• Can bundle courses<br>• Unlimited products<br>• Has membership option<br>• No transaction fees | • Not an all-in-one (no email marketing, no landing pages except for the course sales pages)<br>• Automations are limited<br>• Lack of customization<br>• No SMS functionality (must use third-party platform)<br>• Can't calculate / collect sales tax<br>• Does not support multi-currency |

# Thrivecart Learn

| Pros | Cons |
|---|---|
| • Affordability: $<br>• Free to use if you have Thrivecart<br>• No subscription fee - pay one time for lifetime access<br>• Very simple to use<br>• Can bundle courses on upgraded Learn+ plan (one-time upgrade fee for lifetime access)<br>• Unlimited products<br>• Has membership option<br>• No transaction fees<br>• Can calculate and collect sales tax<br>• Multi-currency per product | • No email marketing<br>• Lack of customization<br>• Does not support multi-currency per product (will have to create separate products per currency) |

# Comparison Tables

| Features & Benefits | ClickFunnels | Kartra | Kajabi |
|---|---|---|---|
| Free Plan | No<br>14-day trial | No<br>14-day trial | No<br>30-day trial |
| Cost | Starts at $97/month | Starts at $99/month | Starts at $149/month |
| All-In-One | ✓ | ✓ | ✓ |
| Bundle Courses | ✓ | ✓ | ✓ |
| Products | Unlimited | Unlimited | Three on basic |
| Drag-and-Drop Editor | ✓ | ✓ | ✓ |
| Custom Domain | ✓ | ✓ | ✓ |
| Emails | On the Full Suite plan | ✓ | ✓ |
| Automations | On the Full Suite plan | Advanced | Basic |
| SMS | ✓ | ✓ | Via Zapier |
| Facebook Messenger | ✓ | Via Zapier | Via Zapier |
| Checkout | ✓ | ✓ | ✓ |
| Collect Sales Tax | Via Third party | ✓ | No |
| Transaction Fees | No | No | No |
| Membership | ✓ | ✓ | ✓ |
| Additional Notes | Mobile optimization | Steeper learning curves | |
| Sign Up | [QR code] | [QR code] | [QR code] |

| Features & Benefits | Podia | Teachable | Thinkific | Thrivecart Learn |
|---|---|---|---|---|
| Free Plan | ✓ | ✓ | ✓ | ✓ |
| Cost | Starts at $39/month | Starts at $59/month | Starts at $49/month | $195 one-time fee for upgrade |
| All-In-One | ✓ | No | No | No |
| Bundle Courses | ✓ | ✓ | ✓ | Learn+ |
| Products | On on free. Unlimited on paid. | Unlimited | Unlimited | Unlimited |
| Drag-and-Drop Editor | ✓ | ✓ | ✓ | ✓ |
| Custom Domain | ✓ | ✓ | ✓ | ✓ |
| Emails | ✓ | ✓ | ✓ | No |
| Automations | ✓ | ✓ | Limited | No |
| SMS | Via Zapier | ✓ | Via Zapier | No |
| Facebook Messenger | Via Zapier | Via Zapier | Via Zapier | No |
| Checkout | ✓ | ✓ | ✓ | ✓ |
| Collect Sales Tax | ✓ | ✓ But not on custom gateway | No | ✓ |
| Transaction Fees | 8% on free, none on paid plans | 10% on free plan, 5% on basic plan | No | No |
| Membership | ✓ | ✓ | ✓ | ✓ |
| Additional Notes | | | | |
| Sign Up | | | | |

# Chapter 14 Questions/Exercises

1. What is the most important feature for you that an online course platform must have? For example, for some businesses, the ability to calculate and collect sales tax is important.

2. What features can you live without?

# Chapter 15: Other Tech Considerations

In addition to the technology you need for email marketing/drip campaigns, landing pages, and courses, you might find yourself in need of additional tech to make your funnel run as smoothly as possible.

## Webinar Platforms

If you've decided to offer webinars, whether live or evergreen (automated webinars that run on-demand), you'll need a system that can help you run your webinars. There are many options available. In this guide, I'll touch on four of them.

## 1. Zoom Meetings

Zoom Meetings is a great affordable option if you are planning to run all of your webinars live. They offer a free option that is limited to 40 minutes for up to 100 attendees. Their paid plans start at $200/year or $20/month, which is super reasonable. If you're on a tight budget, and you don't plan to run a lot of webinars, this might be a good option for you. If you need more than 40 minutes or expect over 100 attendees, you can always upgrade for one month (the month when your webinar takes place), and then downgrade back to the free option for subsequent months. In other words, upgrade when you need to use the upgraded features, and downgrade afterwards to save on costs.

The downside is that you aren't able to do any evergreen webinars using Zoom Meetings. They do have a Webinar option, but there's a minimum of 500 attendees and the cost starts at $918 per year. In my opinion, there are better webinar platforms for that, which I'll touch on next.

## 2. Zoho Meetings or Webinar

Zoho meetings is very similar to Zoom meetings, but their pricing is much more reasonable. Their free plan allows up to 100 participants for up to 60 minutes (in comparison to Zoom's 40-minute limit on their free plan). Their paid plans start under $8 per month (when billed annually). Zoho also has a webinar option that is a lot more cost effective than Zoom. Unlike Zoom's minimum of 500 attendees on their webinar plans, Zoho's minimum is 25 attendees and their plan starts at $112 per year.

You can pre-record your webinar to run as an evergreen webinar, although the features aren't as robust as EasyWebinar or Demio (details on both below).

## 3. EasyWebinar

EasyWebinar is useful for live and evergreen (automated) webinars. You can choose to hold a live webinar and then turn that live webinar into an evergreen one. Some of the features I love about EasyWebinar include:

- Ability to customize your landing page
- Embed registration button on your own landing page
- Ability to customize your thank you page or redirect to your own thank you page
- Ability to customize your pre and post-webinar notifications and emails
- Immediately convert live webinars to evergreen with many different scheduling options
- Option to present your offer at specified times during your webinar

- Integrates with YouTube live and Facebook live

One downside of EasyWebinar, although not a deal breaker in my opinion, is that it can't host the videos on its platform. For automated webinars, you'll need to upload your video to Vimeo or YouTube first in order to use it in EasyWebinar. Just make sure you set your video to viewable using a private link so it is not accessible by anyone just doing a search on Vimeo or YouTube.

EasyWebinar starts at $99/month for up to 100 attendees. They offer a full access free trial for 14 days. Sign up for their 14-day trial using the QR code below.

## 4. Demio

If you're only intending to run live webinars, Demio's live webinar plan starts at $49/month. If you want to do both live and evergreen webinars, their plan starts at $99/month. What I like about this is that you can sign up for the $49/month plan, upgrade when you need to, and then downgrade if you don't need all the extra features. Some of the features I like about Demio are:

- You can host your video directly in Demio so there is no need

to upload it to vimeo or YouTube first
- You can show offers at anytime during your webinar
- You can customize the registration page and embed it on your own website
- You can customize the pre-webinar notification emails to a certain extent

The downside of Demio is that it doesn't have some of the features that EasyWebinar offers such as integration with YouTube live and Facebook live. Sign up for Demio using the QR code below.

## Checkout Cart

If you are selling a service or product, you'll need to accept payment, and there are many different ways to do this. Depending on the platform you've chosen for your email marketing, landing page, and online course, a checkout feature might already be included with the platform. However, from my experience, the checkouts included with those platforms are usually pretty basic. You can also use PayPal and Stripe directly to accept payments, but integrating PayPal or Stripe to move customers to your online course platform can be unnecessarily difficult to do especially if you aren't overly tech savvy.

Something else to consider that people commonly overlook initially is sales tax. Keep in mind that many platforms don't have the ability to add and calculate sales tax, so if tax is something you need to charge, you'll have to consider a checkout platform that can handle tax.

If you'd like to get a little more sophisticated, I really love and highly recommend a platform called Thrivecart. Thrivecart is a mini funnel in and of itself. You can create product bumps and upsells and customize your checkout page to help maximize conversions. One feature I love as a Canadian is the ability to calculate and add sales tax, something that is lacking in other platforms.

Thrivecart also has an online course component called Learn and Learn+, so you can build your online course right in there too.

Thrivecart is an excellent checkout platform with a focus to get your products to convert, and it is reasonably priced as well. There are no monthly fees. You can get lifetime access for $495 (with a pro upgrade for $195). They both include Learn. The Learn+ upgrade is a one-time fee of $195 (in addition to the pro upgrade). I have a feeling this offer won't last (as of February 2024, this offer is part of their pricing), so if you're considering it, I would recommend that you get it before the offer disappears and they start charging monthly. You can sign up for Thrivecart using the QR Code below.

# Zapier

Last but not least on my tech list is a tool called Zapier. This is an essential tool everyone can use. Zapier is a "platform bridge" that helps you connect or integrate two or more platforms or technical elements that don't directly integrate with one another.

For example, if you'd like to add purchases to a Google sheet for internal tracking (or for another internal purpose), you could set up a "zap" to pull the purchases from your payment platform and populate a Google sheet with the purchasers' info.

Another example is, going back to the Email Marketing Comparison Table, if you would like to integrate MailerLite with Facebook lead ads, this would have to be done via Zapier as there isn't a direct integration between the two.

Zapier offers a free version, which for someone just starting out should be sufficient, or a paid plan for more sophisticated integrations.

# Calendar Booking

If your call-to-action is for subscribers to book a meeting or consultation with you, consider an online scheduling or appointment booking platform. An online scheduler simplifies the scheduling process, eliminating the need for manual back-and-forth communication as you try to find suitable time slots.

Here's what an email correspondence might look like when you and a potential client try to schedule a meeting:

> Hi, Jane,
>
> Let's schedule a meeting to further discuss your needs. I'm available at the following days and times:
>
> Monday at 11 a.m., 1 p.m., or 5 p.m.
> Tuesday from 9:30 a.m.-11:30 a.m.
> Friday at 9 a.m. and 10 a.m.
>
> Would any of those work for you?
>
> Best regards,
> John

> Hi, John,
>
> Unfortunately, I can't make any of those work. Here's my availability.
>
> Monday at 2:30 p.m., 6 p.m. and 7 p.m,
> Wednesday from 10 a.m.-12 p.m.
> Friday at 8 a.m., 11 a.m. and 3 p.m.
>
> Please let me know.
>
> Thanks!
> Jane

> Hi, Jane,
>
> I can do Monday from 1:30-2:30 p.m. I know that isn't one of the times you listed, but I do have another meeting at 2:30 p.m. that I can't move. Please let me know if there's any way you can make that time work.
>
> Thanks,
> John

> Hi, John,
>
> I managed to move my other meeting, so, yes, I can do Monday at 1:30 p.m. Is this in PST? I'm in California. Will you send an invite or should I?
>
> Warmly,
> Jane

Does that nightmare sound familiar? Compare that to the following email correspondence using a booking link from a scheduling platform:

> Hi, Jane,
>
> I'd love to have a quick 30-minute meeting to discuss your needs and see how I might be able to help you. Please feel free to schedule a meeting via my calendar: [link].
>
> I'm looking forward to connecting with you.
>
> Best regards,
> John

> Hi, John,
>
> Thanks for sending me your calendar. I've booked a meeting for Monday at 1:30 p.m.
>
> See you then!
>
> Jane

Nice, right? Typically, a calendar booking platform integrates with various calendar systems, such as Google Calendar, Microsoft Outlook, Apple Calendar, or other popular calendars, to provide a seamless experience for both the service provider and their clients or customers. You can also set up automated reminder emails so you don't have to spend time reminding clients of their upcoming meeting with you. And everything is shown in the end user's time zone, making it a seamless interaction. Basically you can set it and forget it!

Below are three online scheduling platforms that I recommend. My top choice is TidyCal because the low one-time payment of $29 (at the time of this publication) gives you lifetime access to all the paid features. You can connect it to multiple calendars and integrate it with Stripe or PayPal to accept payment.

| TidyCal | Acuity | Calendly |
|---|---|---|

# Chapter 15 Questions/Exercises

1. There is a lot of tech to consider when you are setting up a sales funnel. Which of the following additional tech do you think you'll be needing?

- [ ] Webinar platform
- [ ] Checkout cart
- [ ] Integration (Zapier)
- [ ] Calendar/Scheduling software

2. Why do you need the tech that you checked off above?

_____
_____
_____
_____

# Chapter 16: A/B Testing

A/B testing plays an important role in the success of your campaigns. Great marketers are always A/B testing their landing pages and email campaigns. But what is A/B testing? It's a data-driven approach to help you make informed decisions and optimize various elements of your landing page or email campaign (you can also do A/B testing for other aspects of your business). The "A/B" shows that the process is split testing and is exactly like it sounds. You split your landing page or emails into two different versions (or sometimes more)—an A version and a B version—then you test which one performs better. The test is done by randomly assigning visitors to either test A or test B. If the platform you are using has an A/B test function, you won't have to do this manually as it can be done by the system. If it doesn't have an A/B test function, it will take more work on your end to have to create two or more versions of your landing page or email. If this is important to you, I would recommend signing up for the platforms that offer A/B testing as a feature.

## Identify Your Goal

Before you start testing, the first step is to define a specific goal or key performance indicator (KPI) that you want to improve. For example, you might want to increase the click-through rate (CTR) of an email campaign (meaning getting more people to click on one or more links you include in your email) or improve the conversion rate of a landing page so more people sign up. Without a goal, it's hard to understand what you need to test, why you should test, and what is considered a success.

## What Do You Test?

You can test any number of things, but the key is to test one thing at a time. If you test too many variables at once, it's hard to analyze what is working and what isn't. Once you've tested one variable, you can move on and test another variable.

These are the different variables you can test:

## A Different Variation For Your Headline (On a Landing Page) or Subject Line (On an Email)

For example, you can test "The Ultimate Guide To Walking Your Dog with Ease" or "Don't let your dog control you during your walks" and see which headline resonates more with your audience and provides the most positive results.

## Content

For emails, you can test your content. Maybe you want to see if text-based emails or emails with images have a better open or click-through rate. Maybe you want to see if including GIFs in your emails will lead to more engagement. Or perhaps you want to test adding a button for your call-to-action vs. using a simple link. There are various elements you can test in your content, but like everything else, be sure to test only one element at a time.

## Visuals: Imagery and Colors

Visuals play an important role, and often it comes down to choosing the right images and colors. You can test using a different main image or a different button color on your CTA.

## Length of Your Landing Page

The length of your landing page largely depends on the type of landing page you're creating. But it also depends on the awareness level of your brand. If your target audience is highly familiar with your brand, it probably won't take much to convince them to opt-in. However, if they're not aware of your brand, it might take a little more convincing. For example, your webinar opt-in can be very short with just a headline, image, and CTA. Or it can be a little bit longer with information about you as the host, what they'll learn in the webinar, who it's for, and why they should attend. Try testing the two variations and see which one performs best.

## Call-to-Action

Even your CTA copy matters. For example, you can test, "Save Me a Seat!" or "Yes! I want in!" You can test any number of copy variations.

## Timing

Timing matters. While most of us have our phones with us at all times and constantly check our emails, whether we open a specific email or take action will depend on what time of day we receive the email and what we're doing at that time. There are a few companies that analyze the best days and times to send emails, segmented by open and click-through rates. However, these reports are usually quite general as they aren't done by industry. For example, if your target audience is first-time parents who have babies, perhaps you find that the best time to send your audience an email is between 2 a.m.-3 a.m. as they are up doing a night feed, not 10 a.m. when they are busy trying to get their baby to nap or get some chores done during naptime. The point is: get to know your audience. And if you're unsure when the best time is, you can split test the timing of your emails. Try different days and times and see which emails get the most opens and/or click-throughs.

## Analyze Your Tests

If you decide to A/B test, don't forget to analyze the results. There's no sense in A/B testing if you are not analyzing the performance of each test. It's important to note that you don't need to do A/B testing to analyze performance. You should be analyzing regardless of whether you perform any A/B tests. Otherwise, how would you know the success of your funnel if you are not measuring it? At a minimum, most landing page and email marketing platforms will provide the following analytics:

### Landing Page Platforms

- # of views
- # of conversions (form submissions or purchases)

### Email Marketing Platforms

- # of opens
- # of clicks

You can also get more data if you connect your landing page and email marketing platforms to your Google Analytics and Facebook Pixel Accounts. We won't go into too much detail about Google

Analytics and Facebook Pixel in this book, but you can get a ton of information about these two powerful tools and learn about them directly from Google and Facebook:

- Google Analytics: https://analytics.google.com/analytics/academy/course/6
- Facebook Pixel: https://www.facebook.com/gpa/blog/the-facebook-pixel

I find that it's easier to analyze data when the data are all in one location, and I can easily glance at them. I would recommend creating a spreadsheet for all your funnel data so you can analyze the results to determine which version performed better.

Below is an example of a very basic spreadsheet to analyze the same email with two different subject lines.

| Email # | Subject Line | Open Rate | Click-Through Rate | Unsubscribe |
|---|---|---|---|---|
| 1A | Kickstart Your Fitness Journey: Your 7 Game-Changing Strategies Are Inside! | 67.3% | 25% | 0 |
| 1B | Unlock Your Full Potential: 7 Effective Fitness Strategies Inside! | 45.3% | 25% | 2 |

Below is an example of a very basic spreadsheet to analyze the performance of two landing pages that are identical with the exception of the button colors.

| Landing Page | Button Color | Views | Subscribers | Conversion |
|---|---|---|---|---|
| A | Green with white font | 5,257 | 1,252 | 23.8% |
| B | Bright blue with black font | 8,557 | 3,542 | 41.39% |

You can build a similar spreadsheet for any part of your funnel - opt-in page, sales page, email sequence, checkout page, and your ads. As you can see from the examples, by creating a spreadsheet you can easily see which version performed better.

## Chapter 16 Questions/Exercises

1. Do you feel that it's important to A/B test your funnel?

_____
_____
_____
_____

2. It's not recommended to test multiple variables at a time. What is the one variable that you can start testing?

_____
_____
_____
_____

# Chapter 17: Generating Traffic

After your funnel is set up, it's time to generate traffic to your landing page. The purpose of generating traffic is to get in front of your audience. Without an audience, or if your audience can't find you, you don't exist regardless of how good your funnel is!

There are many different ways to generate traffic:

## Social Media

Hopefully you already have a social media presence for your business. If not, it's time you create one. You'll want to focus on the social media platform(s) where your audience hangs out the most. If they are on Instagram, that's where you need to be. If your audience is on

LinkedIn, then create a presence there. If you're not sure where your audience hangs out, it's time to do a bit of research on your target audience.

Not sure where they gather? In the Launch Plan Worksheets, there's a section for Audience where you can identify where your people hang out. Once your funnel is ready, don't be shy. Talk about your offer on your social media channels and tell your audience to go get them. Share your lead magnet whenever you can in the various social media groups you belong to (but make sure business self-promotion posts are allowed before you post).

## Blog

If you have a blog on your website, add a link to your offer in every blog article. This way, when you are promoting your blogs, there's an opportunity for your audience to discover your lead magnet or offer indirectly.

## Collaborate with Social Media Influencers and Larger Businesses

Influencers include bloggers, social media icons, and YouTubers. Find influencers in your niche who target the same audience you do. Approach them to see how you can collaborate with them or if there's a way for you to incentivize them to create content with the purpose of driving traffic to your funnel.

You can also approach larger businesses with a similar audience and suggest collaborations that are mutually beneficial.

## Google My Business

Hopefully, you already have Google My Business (GMB). If you're not sure what this is, GMB is a free online tool provided by Google that allows businesses to manage their online presence on Google including Google Search and Google Maps. It enables businesses to create and update their business profile, interact with customers, and gain insights into their online performance. If you don't already have GMB set up, I highly recommend that you set it up. It's free, and it helps with Search Engine Optimization (SEO is a topic that requires its own book). Post your lead magnet/offer on your GMB account to help customers find it.

## Paid Traffic

Paid advertising is another way to drive traffic to your business. You can do paid ads in Google, Facebook, Instagram, LinkedIn and Bing. There are different paid ads that allow you to do the following:

- Pay-Per-Click (PPC)
- Pay-Per-View
- Display Ads

- Remarketing

If you're not sure how to do paid ads, refer to the Resources section in Chapter 19 for a list of resources that can help you with paid ads.

## Forums

Forums such as Reddit, WikiAnswers and Quora allow users to ask and answer questions from other users. Search for topics related to your business and provide an expert answer, and when possible, provide a link to your lead magnet or offer. You can do this in various Facebook and LinkedIn Groups as well, as long as the rules allow business-related or self-promotion posts.

# Chapter 17 Questions/Exercises

1. There are multiple ways to generate traffic to your funnel. As a start, what do you feel would be the easiest way for you to drive traffic to your business?

2. Do you have a social media presence currently? If so, which platform can you use to generate traffic?

3. What are some free ways you can use to generate traffic?

# Chapter 18: Funnel Maps

In Chapter 3, I covered the different types of funnels you can create. In the next few pages, you'll see sample funnel diagrams for each of the funnels mentioned in Chapter 3. You can use these examples as-is or add to/modify them according to your own needs. For example, you can have fewer or more emails, or you can lead your prospects to another second funnel instead of offering the product at the end of the first funnel.

You can also combine the funnels and move your leads through different funnels to maximize your chances of conversion. Basically, you can be as simple or as advanced as you like. However, if you are just starting with funnels, I recommend keeping it simple and working up to more advanced funnels after you're a bit more experienced, as it might get overwhelming to try working with advanced funnels right away.

## List Building Funnel

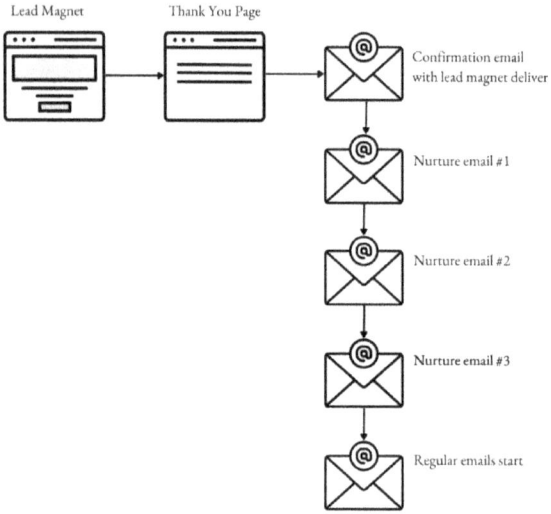

## Free Consultation Funnel

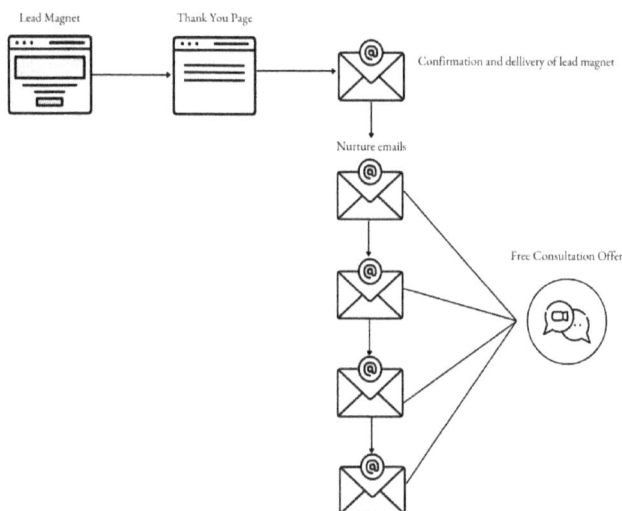

# Product Launch Funnel

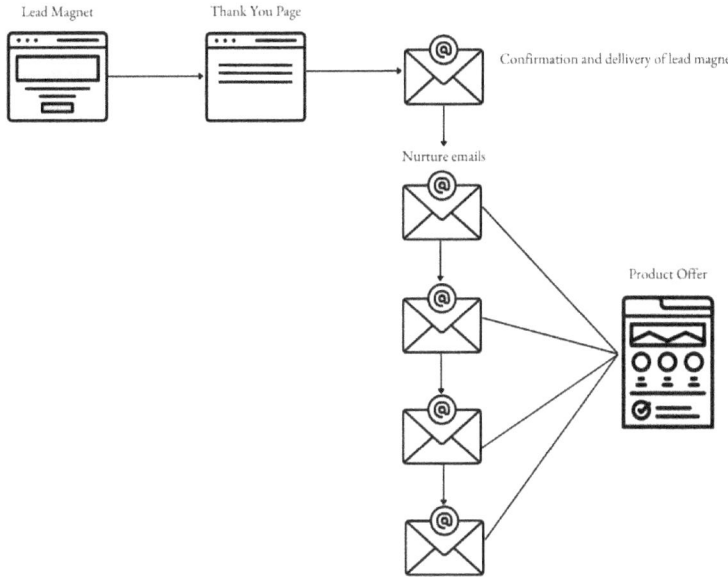

# Webinar Funnel

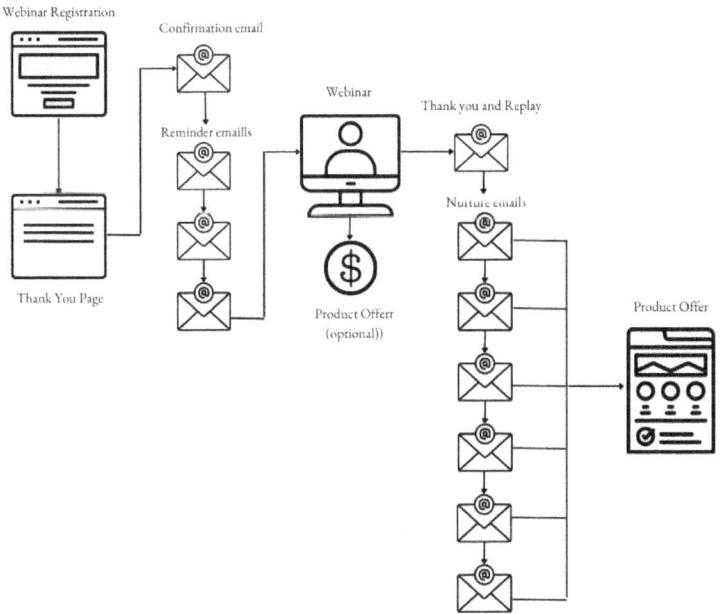

# The Waitlist Funnel

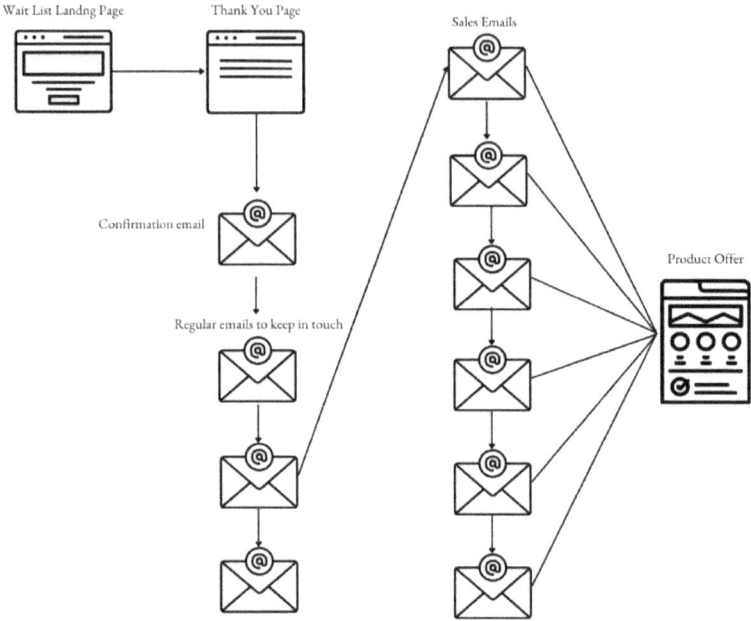

# The Mini Course Funnel

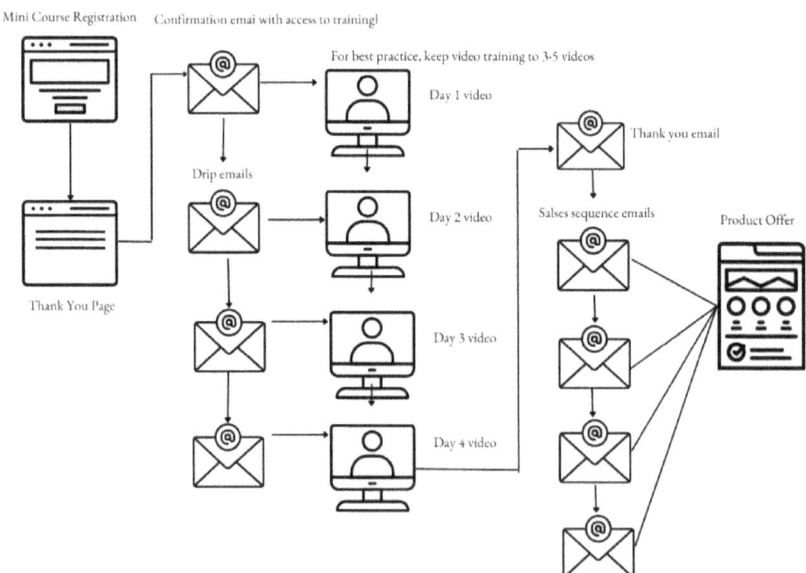

# The Abandoned Cart Funnel

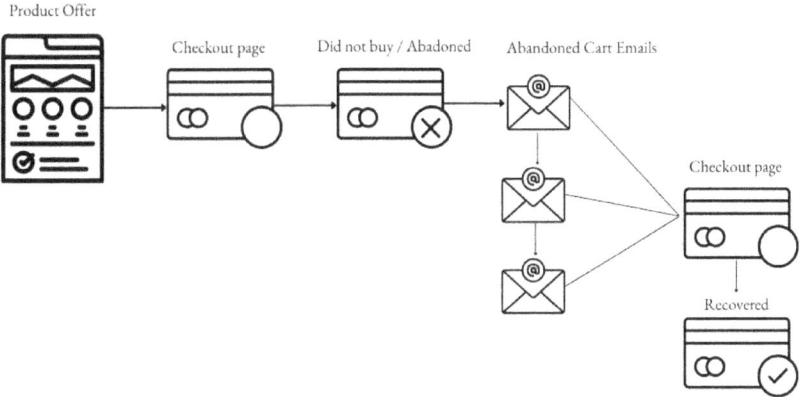

# The Post-Purchase Funnel

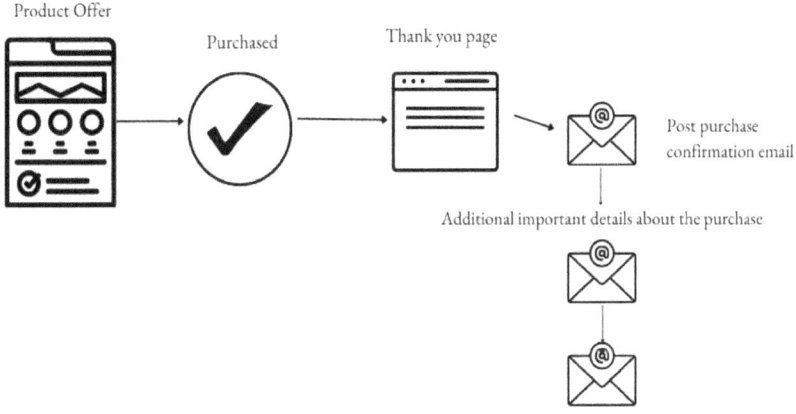

# The Downsell Funnel

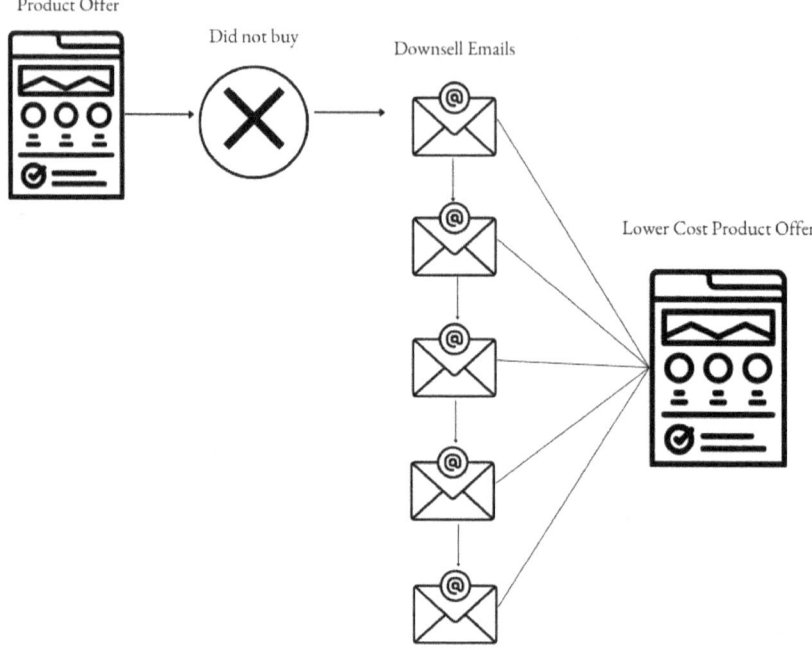

# The Upsell Funnel

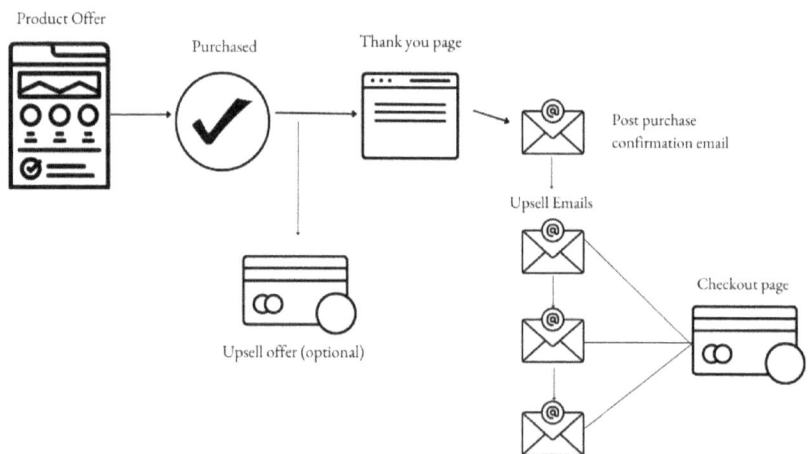

# Combining Your Funnels

If you're just starting out, I would recommend beginning with a basic funnel. You can't go wrong with either a list-building funnel or the product launch funnel if you already have a product you want to sell. As you gain more experience with funnel setups, you can combine your funnels to create more advanced ones. Below are some combinations you can consider. The combinations can be endless!

1. List building funnel + free consultation funnel
2. Waitlist funnel (with no product launch) + Webinar funnel
3. Product launch funnel + abandoned cart funnel
4. Product launch funnel + abandoned cart funnel + upsell funnel
5. Product launch funnel + abandoned cart funnel + downsell funnel + upsell funnel
6. List building + mini course funnel
7. List building + waitlist funnel (no product) + mini course funnel + abandoned cart funnel + downsell funnel + upsell funnel

Here's an example of a funnel combination

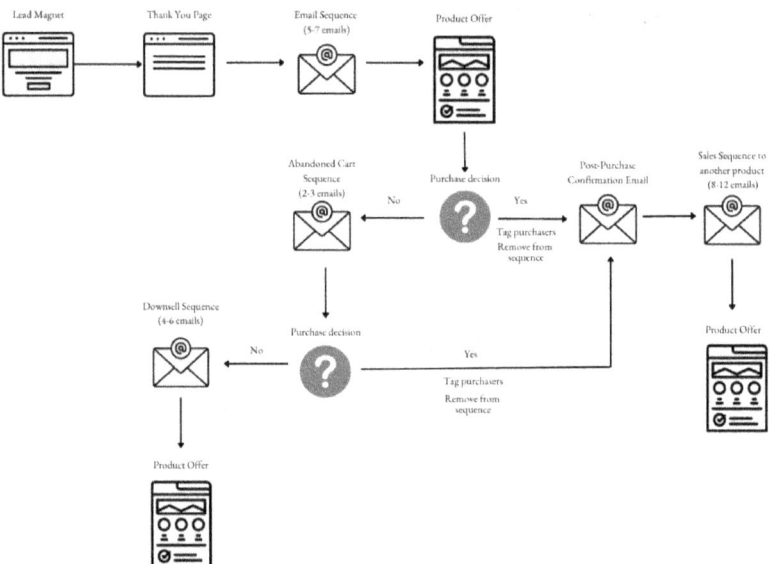

If your head is exploding/eyes are crossing at the thought of having to build all these funnels yourself, don't worry - in the Resources section, you'll find a link to book a consultation with me, along with other funnel experts who can help you including copywriters and a Facebook Ads strategist.

# Chapter 18 Questions/Exercises

1. Name one common element in all of these funnel maps.

_____
_____
_____
_____

2. Are list building and waitlist funnels different or the same, and why?

_____
_____
_____
_____

3. What is the difference between an upsell and a downsell funnel? Which one would you use for your funnel and why?

_____
_____
_____
_____

# Chapter 19: Recommended Resources

Having the right resources is an important part of building your funnel. This section lists all of the recommended resources you can use to help you with your setup. You can also find all of this information on my website at digitalpixie.ca/resources, or you can scan the QR code below for easy access.

I will also recommend you join my mailing list where I regularly send out useful information on new tech, systems, and strategies for business owners. Visit digitalpixie.ca/mailinglist or scan the QR codes heres.

| Resources | Mailing List |
|---|---|
| [QR code] | [QR code] |

## Copywriters

As I mentioned in earlier chapters, your copy is crucial to your conversion rate. It's imperative that you understand your audience and can emotionally connect with them. You may be a great writer; however, more importantly, can you write copy that converts?

There are many different types of writing. You may be able to write for a specific purpose or genre, but you'll need to be honest with yourself as to whether you are skilled in the art of selling without sounding like you're selling.

Your copy can make or break your funnel. That's why if copywriting for funnels isn't your area of expertise, I suggest you outsource the copywriting to an expert. Below is a list of trusted copywriters I have worked with and heartily recommend (in no particular order).

1. **Jill Wise** - digitalpixie.ca/resources/jillwise

    Use coupon code ASTRID10 to get $10 off Jill's Canned Email Templates

2. **Sara Vartanian** - digitalpixie.ca/resources/saravartanian

Use coupon code ASTRIDS to get 15% off all copy products

3. **One Lit Place** - digitalpixie.ca/resources/onelitplace

   Use coupon code ASTRID15 to get 15% off all writing coaching, copywriting, and editing hours and/or their Website Copywriting Package

## Content Creation:

1. **Danielle Lewis Designs** - digitalpixie.ca/resources/daniellelewisdesigns

   Use code ASTRIDS to get 10% off Danielle's graphic design services for your lead magnet

2. **Maverick Makers** - video creation, editing and on-camera training - digitalpixie.ca/maverickmakers

   Use code ASTRIDS to get 15% of Maverick Makers services

3. **Canva** - free online design software: digitalpixie.ca/resources/canva

4. **Unsplash** - free stock photos: digitalpixie.ca/resources/unsplash

5. **Pexels** - free stock photos: digitalpixie.ca/resources/pexels

6. **Pixabay** - free stock photos: digitalpixie.ca/resources/pixabay

7. **Free images** - free stock photos: digitalpixie.ca/resources/freeimages

8. **Shutterstock** - premium stock photos: digitalpixie.ca/

resources/shutterstock

9. **iStock** - premium stock photos: digitalpixie.ca/resources/istock

# Facebook and Instagram Ads

Facebook and Instagram ads can be a very effective way to generate traffic to your funnel. Now, can you run your own ads? Absolutely! But just like copywriting, if ad creation and management isn't your area of expertise, I would suggest you hire an expert or, at the very least, learn to do it yourself the right way. Facebook ads can seem simple, but if they aren't done right, you'll just end up spending money on ads that won't convert.

Trust me when I say that it isn't easy to find a Facebook Ads agency who is truly great at what they do. That's why I recommend working with Alvaro Berrios Digital for your Facebook Ads or taking his Facebook Ads courses.

1. **Facebook Ads Ignition** - digitalpixie.ca/resources/adsignition
2. **Facebook Ads Rapid Launch** - digitalpixie.ca/resources/rapidlaunch
3. **Facebook Ads Jumpstart Foundations** - digitalpixie.ca/resources/jumpstart
4. **Facebook Ads Consultation** - digitalpixie.ca/resources/alvaroberrios - free one-hour session only for our readers (a

$300 value). Mention ASTRID SUCIPTO to claim this offer (limited sessions available while supplies last).

## Opt-In Forms and Email Automation

You can use many platforms to capture lead information and send out automated emails. Refer back to the email marketing tools comparison chart in Chapter 11 to see what the platforms are and their features.

The following is not a comprehensive list by any means (there are a ton out there!). I've also included some additional ones that aren't on the comparison chart. I recommend MailerLite because they have the best price point and the greatest functionality, but you can choose whichever tool suits your needs.

1. **MailerLite** - digitalpixie.ca/resources/mailerlite
2. **ConvertKit** - digitalpixie.ca/resources/convertkit
3. **ActiveCampaign** - digitalpixie.ca/resources/activecampaign
4. **MailChimp** - digitalpixie.ca/resources/mailchimp
5. **Constant Contact** - digitalpixie.ca/resources/constantcontact
6. **Drip** - digitalpixie.ca/resources/drip
7. **AWeber** - digitalpixie.ca/resources/aweber
8. **Flodesk** - digitalpixie.ca/resources/flodesk
9. **SendFox** - digitalpixie.ca/resources/sendfox
10. **Brevo** - digitalpixie.ca/resources/brevo

## Landing Pages

There are many landing page platforms. Refer back to the landing page comparison chart in Chapter 10 to see the platforms and their features. The following is not a comprehensive list.

1. **MailerLite** - digitalpixie.ca/resources/mailerlite
2. **Leadpages** - digitapixie.ca/resources/leadpages
3. **Instapage** - digitalpixie.ca/resources/instapage
4. **Wishpond** - digitalpixie.ca/resources/wishpond
5. **Unbounce** - digitalpixie.ca/resources/unbounce

## Quiz Building Platform

1. **Interact** - digitalpixie.ca/resources/interact

## Course Platforms

1. **Podia** - digitalpixie.ca/resources/podia
2. **Thrivecart Learn** - digitalpixie.ca/resources/thrivecart
3. **Thinkific** - digitalpixie.ca/resources/thinkific
4. **Teachable** - digitalpixie.ca/resources/teachable

## All-In-One Platforms

All-in-one platforms usually include the following capabilities: landing page builder, email marketing and automation, list building, form builder, and online course hosting.

1. **Kajabi** - digitalpixie.ca/resources/kajabi

2. **Kartra** - digiralpixie.ca/resources/kartra

3. **ClickFunnels** - digitalpixie.ca/resources/clickfunnels

## Webinar Platforms

1. **Zoom** - digitalpixie.ca/resources/zoom

2. **Zoho** - digitalpixie.ca/resources/zoho

3. **EasyWebinar** - digitalpixie.ca/resources/easywebinar

4. **Demio** - digitalpixie.ca/resources/demio

## Booking Calendar

1. **TidyCal** - digitalpixie.ca/resources/tidycal

2. **Calendly** - digitalpixie.ca/resources/calendly

3. **Acuity** - digitalpixie.ca/resources/acuity

## Other Good to Have Tech

1. **Zapie**r - digitalpixie.ca/resources/zapier

2. **Thrivecart** - digitalpixie.ca/resources/thrivecart

## Consultation

Last but not least, for funnel-building advice, support on how to build your funnel, or other questions, I am available for consultations at digitalpixie.ca/consultation. You can also scan the QR code here.

# Chapter 20: Launch Plan Worksheets (Recommended)

## Why do you need a launch plan?

"By failing to plan, you are preparing to fail"

-Benjamin Franklin

Let's say you're planning a road trip from Toronto to New York. Do you just get in a car and start driving without any sense of which direction to go in? Probably not. You have to plan your route in advance to know where you're going; otherwise, you'll get lost and maybe never get to your destination. Or maybe you will eventually, but it will have cost you a lot of wasted time and money.

It works the same way with funnels. You have to have a start, an end goal, and a plan to get you to your destination. Without knowing where you're going or the route you're going to take, you might be spinning your wheels. This is where our Launch Plan Worksheets come in. They're the secret to planning a solid funnel strategy.

## What's included in the Sales Mastery Launch Plan Worksheets?

### Preliminary Planning Worksheet

Planning is a vital component of any project. Not only does it help you identify what you need in advance, it keeps the process manageable and measured as you build the elements that will help you succeed. In this worksheet, we'll identify your client avatar, audience, your goal, and more.

### Mapping Out Your Funnel

In this worksheet, you'll identify the funnel that you want to create and map it out so you can visualize the process flow to ensure that you have everything you need for your funnel.

### Your Freebie Worksheet

Use this worksheet to come up with your perfect freebie.

### Landing Page Checklist

This checklist helps you work out the elements you need for your landing page.

## Landing Page Copywriting Worksheet

The copy on your lading page is crucial to its success or lack thereof. Use the worksheet to help you write copy that converts. If copywriting isn't your skillset, I recommend you outsource it. The completed worksheet will help your copywriter understand how to write your content for you.

## Landing Page Wireframe Templates

Use this worksheet to help you structure and build your landing page.

## Nurture Emails Worksheet

While your landing page is important for capturing leads, your nurture emails are critical for turning them into paying customers. Take your time with this. Go through the worksheet and dig deep to understand who you are writing these emails to and what you are writing about. Once you've done the worksheet, jump into the Nurture Emails template for guidance and examples. You can then use the Email Worksheet to help you structure each of your nurture emails.

## Nurture Emails Template

Use this template to help you write your nurture emails. The better your emails are, the more chance you have of converting your audience. Keep in mind that your customers are probably bombarded with emails all day every day. The template will get you to think of ways to capture your audience's attention through your emails.

### Creating Your Online Course Worksheet

If creating an online course is a goal that you have, this worksheet can help you work through it to build the bones of your course.

### Tech Stack and Checklist: Connecting The Steps and Stacking Your Systems

This checklist helps you understand what steps are needed to set up a funnel on the back end (what happens behind the scenes) and front end (what people see). Keep this checklist handy as you work on setting up your funnel.

## Special Discount

Access these worksheets for only $17 when you apply the code "MochaLatte". Head over to my website: digitalpixie.ca/worksheets to download and print the worksheets. Your funnel success awaits!

# ACKNOWLEDGMENTS

This book started as a short guide many years ago with only a few worksheets, which I sold online as PDFs. Over the years, I've come to realize that business owners need a broader and more extensive guide that walks them through the entire process. I started working on expanding the content, and then I couldn't stop. There's so much information I wanted to share. I know there are many entrepreneurs trying to cobble pieces of their funnel together without having a full understanding of what a funnel is and how to create one effectively. The result is wasted effort, time, and money. I really wanted to create a comprehensive resource that entrepreneurs could refer to over and over again as their primary resource.

I remember working on the guide at a cottage one summer. My family was all outside, including my two little girls, who were about two and four years old at the time, while I sat inside working away at my laptop. There have also been many nights since then when I would watch a movie with my family with my laptop on my lap. So for that, I would like to thank my family (my husband, Edgar, and my two daughters, Averie and Evette) from the bottom of my heart for their understanding, their unending support, and unconditional love during the many hours I spent writing this book and in general. Thank you for being my rock and champion, for always cheering me on. I love you all! I wouldn't be where I am today without you.

I would also like to thank all my business colleagues and partners I've worked on funnels with over the years including Alvaro Berrios, Sara Vartanian, and Jill Wise. Not to mention all of my clients (you know who you are) who have trusted me to build their funnels for them. Watching you launch your offers is incredibly satisfying for me. But what I've loved best was getting to know your businesses more intimately, including your mission to serve as many people as possible in your unique way. I also want to thank all the business owners and entrepreneurs who read this book prior to publication and had such wonderful things to say about it. Reading your reviews and testimonials made my day. Of course, it goes without saying that a thanks is also in order for every staff member and independent contractor who has helped me over the years with client projects.

Whether you are a good writer or not, every writer needs an editor, and for that, I thank my friend, business colleague, and editor, Jenna Kalinsky from One Lit Place. Thank you for being my second set of eyes and for brainstorming different ideas with me. Without you, this book wouldn't be as polished as it is right now.

Last but not least, thank you to you, my readers. I hope that this book has been helpful to you and that you can use it as a resource when you want to build all your sales funnels. Now, go out there and plan your launch!

# ABOUT THE AUTHOR

Astrid Sucipto is the Chief Pixie at Digital Pixie, a boutique Digital Marketing Agency focusing on sales funnels and marketing technology. She has been in the marketing world for 13+ years, starting out in traditional marketing and moving into the digital realm. She is a funnel tech expert and has become the go-to and trusted expert on anything and everything related to digital marketing tools and technology.

Astrid is also a mortgage agent. When she isn't helping businesses with their funnels, she is helping individuals achieve their dreams of home ownership.

As much as Astrid is an entrepreneur, she is a mom first. Her husband and two daughters are her world and her why. She loves being a mom and watching her girls learn and grow. She is also a mom of five feline babies. In her spare time (which isn't much!), she enjoys leather crafting and making skincare products.

www.ingramcontent.com/pod-product-compliance
Lightning Source LLC
Chambersburg PA
CBHW052138070526
44585CB00017B/1885